GLOBAL
GOVERNANCE
REFORM

GLOBAL GOVERNANCE REFORM

Breaking the Stalemate

COLIN I. BRADFORD JR.
JOHANNES F. LINN

EDITORS

BROOKINGS INSTITUTION PRESS
Washington, D.C.

Library of Congress Cataloging-in-Publication data
Global governance reform : breaking the stalemate / Colin I. Bradford and Johannes F.
Linn, editors.
    p.   cm.
  Summary: "Explores a wide range of challenges facing the international community in
reforming international institutions and global governance groups. Argues for reform of
global governance groups, especially reconstituting the G-8, and individual institutional
reforms in the IMF, World Bank, and the United Nations and in global health and
environmental governance."—Provided by publisher.
  Includes bibliographical references and index.
  ISBN-13: 978-0-8157-1363-0 (pbk. : alk. paper)
  ISBN-10: 0-8157-1363-0 (pbk. : alk. paper)
  1. International organization. 2. International cooperation. I. Bradford, Colin I., Jr.
II. Linn, Johannes F.
  JZ1318.G5165 2006
  341.2—dc22   2006038559

9 8 7 6 5 4 3 2 1

The paper used in this publication meets minimum requirements of the
American National Standard for Information Sciences—Permanence of Paper for
Printed Library Materials: ANSI Z39.48-1992.

Typeset in Adobe Garamond

Composition by Peter Lindeman
Arlington, Virginia

Printed by R. R. Donnelley
Harrisonburg, Virginia

Contents

Foreword

STROBE TALBOTT

Governance has been at the core of the Brookings agenda since the institution was founded ninety years ago. In those days, the word referred almost exclusively to national governance. As time went on—and in particular after World War II—the concept was broadened to include global governance. A Brookings scholar, Leo Pasvolsky, played an instrumental role in designing the structure of the United Nations. Today, international institutions face major challenges. This volume of essays by noted experts in their field looks at both specific institutions and the international system as a whole. Its unique contribution lies precisely in that it examines the interaction between the individual institutions and the system and explores their interdependence. In doing so, the book calls on specific groups of professionals to become more aware of the linkages among issues, institutions, and reforms as they work the vineyards of their own expertise.

Foreign finance ministry officials have responsibility for their countries' relations with the international financial institutions—the International Monetary Fund and the World Bank, for example—and foreign ministry officials have responsibility for their countries' interactions with the United Nations. Even though many of the issues addressed by the international financial institutions and the UN overlap, by and large these institutions and the UN exist in separate worlds run by separate groups of people who barely know each other, much less have a common organizational language or culture.

Ronald Waldman, a public health expert and a medical doctor, called himself a "stranger in a strange land" while participating in the conference, attended primarily by economists and finance ministry officials, that generated this volume. But what is gripping about Waldman's observation is that it applies both ways. When Waldman presented his ideas on global health governance and Daniel Esty offered his ideas on global environmental governance (see chapters 7 and 8 in this volume), it was the economists and finance officials who became the "strangers in a strange land." These different groups of people are not used to being in the same room, they are not used to working together, and they are not used to looking beyond their own expertise or institutional setting.

And yet globalization defines, as never before, the interconnectedness of issues, institutions, and actions. And as the economists and finance ministry officials listened to Waldman and Esty, it became clear not only that the problems of governance faced in the global health and environment fields are extraordinarily similar but also that there are clear parallels between those problems and governance issues in the international financial institutions and the UN. It also became clear that even if reforms to improve the capacity of the IMF, the World Bank, and the UN were successful—a tall order indeed—the organization of the international system would still be inadequate to address global health and environmental problems without reforms to improve the governance of international health and environmental institutions. Conversely, it was clear that even if global health and environmental governance reforms were successful, the capacity to deal with health and environmental challenges would be hampered without reforms at the IMF, World Bank, and UN. Accordingly, the major threads and themes in this volume illustrate the linkages among issues, and those linkages define the current system as literally a system in crisis. That is in part because the connections have been ignored and in part because communication takes place within isolated channels, not between institutions, seriously hampering effective reform and advances.

This volume is based on a series of seminars held at Brookings in the winter and spring of 2006 attended by Washington-based officials from various embassies and national delegations to the IMF and the World Bank. Those officials, representing twenty countries, engaged in a policy dialogue on specific reform issues in the IMF, the World Bank, the United Nations, the G-20 finance ministers group, the ministerial committees of the bank and the IMF, and the global health institutions. In May 2006 an off-the-record conference of officials from both the finance and the foreign ministries of fifteen countries engaged in a two-day conversation about both specific institutional reforms and general global governance issues, with special attention to summit reform—that is, expanding the G-8 into a forum that is more inclusive and representative of the rest of the world.

This volume draws on both the seminar series and the conference, pulling together papers written by the participants. This book is written in nontechnical, jargon-free language to facilitate communication across disciplines, professions, and specialties. The overall message is clear: it is vital to move forward, both within specific institutions and in global governance, if the international system is to be up to the task of giving practical meaning to the phrase "international community."

STROBE TALBOTT
President

Washington, D.C.
December 2006

Acknowledgments

This book is the product of a three-year long collaboration with the Centre for International Governance Innovation (CIGI) in Waterloo, Ontario, Canada. Without doubt, we owe our deepest debt of gratitude to John English, executive director, and Andrew Cooper, associate director, for their interest and involvement in our undertakings and their support of and contributions to our activities. For three years, under their leadership, CIGI has provided financial support for the series of roundtables, seminars, and conferences that we have organized at Brookings to involve Washington-based officials from G-20 countries and others in examining the issues of global governance reform that led to this book. It has been a pleasure for us to work with both of them.

We also are grateful to Strobe Talbott, president of Brookings, and Jim Balsillie, board chairman of CIGI, for their growing interest in broadening and deepening the Brookings-CIGI collaboration and for their increasing involvement in this partnership.

The Centre for Global Studies (CFGS) at the University of Victoria in Victoria, British Columbia, Canada, also with collaborative support from CIGI, has carried out an extensive series of conferences on issues that expanded summits might address in a reformed global governance format.

We are extremely grateful to Gordon Smith, director, and Barry Carin, associate director, for their collaboration with us and especially for their financial support of and involvement in our May 4–5, 2006, conference, the results of which have been a key input into this book.

In the fall of 2003, Carol Graham, then vice president of Governance Studies at Brookings, brought both of us into Brookings as visiting fellows. As it happened, our offices were steps away from each other. That coincidence facilitated numerous exchanges that ultimately led to our joining forces in generating the activities that resulted in this book. We are both extremely indebted to Carol for her generous invitation and support for our individual and collaborative work. Without her initiative, none of this would have transpired. More recently, Lael Brainard, vice president of Global Economy and Development at Brookings, has been extremely supportive of our project and has provided a welcome home for it and for the new Wolfensohn Center.

We also are grateful to numerous Brookings colleagues who have been good enough to participate in our activities, to give us guidance, and to comment on our research and writing. We would like to mention particularly Bill Antholis, Ralph Bryant, Susan Collins, Ken Dam, Bill Frenzel, Ann Florini, Carlos Pascual, Lex Rieffel, and Jim Steinberg for their much appreciated colleagueship. We also appreciate the excellent editorial work of Eileen Hughes at the Brookings Institution Press and the overall guidance on the publication of this book offered by Janet Walker and Chris Kelaher.

Massachusetts Avenue in Washington is home to a number of think tanks and a place where the excellence of individual institutions combines with that of others to create a still larger impact on ideas in the policy community. We are grateful to our friends and colleagues at the Institute for International Economics and the Center for Global Development, across the street from Brookings, for their participation in our work. We are especially grateful to Fred Bergsten, Ted Truman, and John Williamson at IIE and Nancy Birdsall, Dennis de Tray, and Ruth Levine at CGD for their involvement in this endeavor.

We want to acknowledge here the more than one hundred officials from G-20 countries who have participated in our policy dialogues and thank them for their interest and involvement. They and their peers and colleagues in the capitals of G-20 countries are the primary audience for this work, which we hope in some way will contribute to accelerating action on both international institutional and global governance reform.

We would like to express our appreciation to the other authors in this volume, first for their experience and expertise, which enabled them to make such significant contributions, and second for having the good will and taking the time to prepare, edit, and review their chapters.

Finally, each of us would like to thank Jim Wolfensohn, who provided distinguished leadership in international development as president of the World Bank during the period immediately before we came to Brookings and who has given so generously to Brookings as a trustee and now as founder of the new Wolfensohn Center. He was an inspiration to each of us, who had quite different career trajectories, prior to our coming to Brookings, and we are grateful to him for making the Wolfensohn Center a reality within the Brookings setting.

For readers who may wish to pursue further the issues raised in this book, we recommend visiting the websites of the three sponsoring organizations: Brookings (www.brookings.edu), under Wolfensohn Center for Development; CIGI (www.cigionline.ca), under Research; and CFGS (www.globalcentres.org), under Programs. See also www.l20.org. In addition, a new international network called IGLOO, which is composed of individuals and organizations focused solely on finding innovative solutions to global governance challenges, provides additional research and information resources. See www.igloo.org and www.igloo.org/l20project.

GLOBAL
GOVERNANCE
REFORM

Introduction and Overview

COLIN I. BRADFORD JR. AND JOHANNES F. LINN

On January 9, 2006, the lead editorial in the *Washington Post*, entitled "Globalization's Deficit," surveyed the World Trade Organization, the North American Free Trade Agreement, the International Monetary Fund, the World Bank, the G-8, the United Nations, and NATO and found that they "have run out of forward momentum" and that "the stalling of international institutions is striking—and troubling." Those comments suggest that the international system of institutions is inadequate to the tasks of the twenty-first century, tasks that have changed dramatically with the advent of globalization. Moreover, most of today's global institutions were created in the middle of the twentieth century. Since then, the global balance of power has shifted—and will continue to shift—significantly as China, India, and the other emerging market economies gain relative economic strength.

To discuss reform prospects in selected international institutions and their implications for global governance in a rapidly changing world, we—the editors of this volume—organized a series of seminars that ran from November 2005 through April 2006 involving Washington-based officials from twenty countries and a small number of academic and think tank representatives. The seminars, which were sponsored by the Brookings Institution in partnership with two Canadian think tanks, the Centre for International Governance Innovation (CIGI) and the Centre for Global Studies (CFGS), also focused on G-8 summit reform. ˙

We started by addressing the questions of whether and how to expand the number of countries attending the annual summit meetings currently held under the auspices of the G-8. In our view, such an expansion would broaden the representativeness of the countries participating in the annual G-8 leader's summit, which tries to address global challenges and issues in a visible and influential way. A suitably expanded summit could then become the apex institution for global governance. But clearly, summit reform is not enough. So our seminars also considered reform of individual international institutions—in particular, the United Nations, the International Monetary Fund (IMF), the World Bank, and the ministerial committees governing the latter two organizations—as well as the need for governance reform in two globally significant sectors, health and the environment.

As the seminar series moved forward, we became increasingly aware that the reform agendas within the individual international institutions could not be sensibly discussed in isolation from each other. We therefore organized a two-day conference, held May 4–5, 2006, of a large and diverse group of experts and officials from foreign ministries and finance ministries to reflect on the connections, disconnections, dynamics, and spillover effects of action or inaction within key international institutions—for the institutions themselves and the international system. The conference was designed to look for opportunities to break the "stalling" of the institutions and the stalemate in reform by identifying critical factors and issues that present both possibilities and problems for reform and by exploring the potential for a "grand bargain" that might emerge from the individual pieces of the reform puzzle to help move forward on several fronts simultaneously. The uniqueness of this line of inquiry was its focus on the links and interactions between reform of international institutions and reform of global governance—the nexus of global reform efforts.

Four Overarching Conclusions on the Nexus of Global Governance Reform

The chapters in this volume are based on the presentations of the panelists and the discussion among participants in both the seminar series and the conference. They reveal that each domain—each sector and institution and each global governance forum and group, whether the UN Security Council, the international financial institutions, the G-8, or the G-20—is a microcosm unto itself. Each has its own mandate and mission; its own professional language and organizational culture; and its own bureaucratic concerns, difficulties, and hopes, which preoccupy its participants and enclose them in separate worlds. This volume contains chapters written by experienced practitioners and researchers, most of whom have been both actors and ideas people in one of these domains, who know their domain intimately. They were thrown together by the Brookings-CIGI-CFGS policy dialogue, listening to each other and to officials from foreign and finance ministries of major countries. That process resulted in four major conclusions.

First, as Ronald Waldman so aptly put it, each felt like a "stranger in a strange land" when participants from other domains were talking. The process revealed the parochialism of each microcosm and the insularity that can result from focusing exclusively on what goes on inside a single domain and giving limited or no attention to the porous perimeters. It is the interfaces between domains where many of the world's challenges define themselves today. The interaction of "strangers" revealed the degree to which, despite the particularity of each "strange land," global issues generate common challenges for each domain. The process made it clear that they were not such strangers after all and that there is now a critical need to pay attention to the perimeters of each domain and to create more opportunities for interaction across them as a means of addressing global challenges. This is a major finding and one with the potential to increase hopes for common action.

Second, readers of this volume will find that most authors, each writing on a specific institution or issue, arrive at a similar conclusion: reform within a single domain will not happen by actions taken within that domain alone because there are too many conflicting forces, contradictions, and complexities to permit decisive action. Whether it is the excruciating difficulty of moving percentage-point slivers of voting shares in the IMF and the World Bank from Belgium to Brazil or expanding the number of permanent members of the UN Security Council, the forces against reform are daunting indeed. Clearly, participants from each domain shared the sense that the reform process within their domain was "stuck" or "stalled" and that an additional push is needed to break the stalemate.

Third, there was general agreement that the new reality of changed and still changing global economic and demographic weights among key countries and regions requires a rebalancing of the vote and voice, or the shares and chairs, in each of the major international institutions and forums. This issue is front and center at the moment in the debates about the governance of the international financial institutions (IFIs), about the composition of the UN Security Council, and about the membership of the G-8. While this is by no means the only issue in global governance that needs to be resolved, it is at the core of the debate about the legitimacy of global institutions and central to the question of whether an effective global governance framework can be put in place for the next half-century.

Fourth, as a result of the first three conclusions, authors in this volume agree that to break the current stalemate will require a summit-level forum that carries the weight not just of experts and high-level panels, but of the highest political authorities from major countries, who must forge proposals for reform that can drive a broader consensus and eventual reform actions.

In sum, the need for action above and across each domain is clear, as is seen in Jack Boorman's idea of designing reforms that are "congruent" in their politics and content; in Nancy Birdsall's sense of the need to get the members of "the club" constituting the World Bank to act together; in the despair of Ann Florini and Carlos Pascual regarding UN reform; in Ronald Waldman's picture of the fragmented global health governance structure; and in Daniel Esty's description of the degree of nongovernance on the environment.

Thus the common challenges facing specific sectors and institutions generated by global issues define themselves ultimately as intersectorial and interinstitutional challenges and thus require systemwide strategic guidance. Because the complexities and contradictions within institutions severely constrain decisive action and the feasibility of sufficient reform by the institutions themselves, there is a compelling need for summit reform to drive, oversee, and steer international institutional reform.

These common conclusions were not prearranged or urged upon the authors. Rather, they emerged from the participants' own experience, research, and deep concern for the state of global affairs and their shared recognition, reflected throughout this volume, that without major changes across the international system the world will move backward instead of forward and the human condition will worsen rather than improve. These shared concerns about the urgency and importance of undertaking systemic and institutional reform together provide the fundamental thematic threads and content uniting the chapters into a book about the world that we live in and the choices that our societies and governments face. These choices will determine the future of the international governance system, on which the global human condition depends.

Reform of International Institutions

A major focus of discussion at both the seminar series and the conference, and hence in this volume, was reform of international financial institutions (IFIs) and especially of the International Monetary Fund, which has been at the center of recent debates about IFI reform. A few principal issues stand out.

CHAIRS AND SHARES. Many have argued that the current distribution of voting power and the representational structure of the executive boards of the IMF and the World Bank are based on a post–World War II formula that is now obsolete. Proposals abound for changing the structure of "chairs and shares" by changing the formula reflecting the economic weight of member countries, but agreement is tediously difficult to achieve.[1] Nevertheless, persistent pressure for reform continues to come from many quarters, not least the G-20 finance ministers, who issued an enjoinder in October 2005 calling for IMF reform action by the time of the IMF–World Bank fall 2006 meeting, and the International Monetary and Financial Committee (IMFC) ministers, who had issued a similar call already in a communiqué in April 2005. Ralph Bryant and Jack Boorman argue that if there is a change in the chairs-and-shares formula in operational institutions like the World Bank and the IMF, the consultative bodies like the annual G-8 summits should be reformed in a similar, "congruent" fashion. Bryant finds that using multiple-country constituencies, which occupy seventeen of the twenty-four chairs on the IFI boards, have been useful in IFI governance and proposes extending the constituency approach to global consultative bodies such as the "Camdessus councils" (discussed below) and the annual summits.[2]

There are other ways to allocate voting shares besides employing formulas using economic and social weights. Voting in the Global Environment Fund (GEF) and in the trust funds for global public goods, which are housed in the World Bank, employs a distinctive voting share arrangement derived from the varying country contributions to the different funds or uses a double-majority approach that also gives weight to the number of members of the organization.[3] Those arrangements could be discussed as analogues for new arrangements in other institutions.

LEADERSHIP SELECTION. Another IFI reform issue that also has broader implications is the question of who selects the president of the World Bank and the managing director of the IMF. Currently, the United States nominates, historically without opposition, the president of the World Bank, and the European nations agree among themselves on a nominee to be managing director of the IMF, although their choice has in some cases run into opposition. Although the Europeans do have the initiative in choosing the head of the IMF, on three occasions non-Europeans have been considered for the position. There is no doubt that comparable talent exists in other countries to undertake these important posts, but there is some question of whether candidates should be restricted to citizens from the creditor countries that provide the most resources and have the most influence. However, the choice of an experienced former official from Turkey to run the United Nations Development Program (UNDP) and a former top official from Mexico to lead the Organization for Economic Cooperation and Development (OECD) are signs that reform with respect to the selection of leaders of international institutions is already under way. One way to widen the pool of candidates might be to consider the leadership of some of the major international organizations together and to sequence the rotation of leadership by region in order to provide greater regional balance and more equity in regional representation at the top of the international system. This introduces regions as a factor in global governance decisions, a change that could have repercussions for summit reform and other issues.

IFI COUNCILS. Michel Camdessus has proposed creating councils of ministers for both the World Bank and the IMF that would, together with heads of state at the summit level, provide strategic guidance for each institution and for their relations with one another and with other international organizations.[4] Creating such councils would lead to a new arrangement linking a reformed heads-of-state summit with the councils of ministers and the boards of governors for each institution in order to guide senior management and the executive boards on the broad direction and policy goals of the IFIs. That would replace the current chain of command involving the boards of governors, the bank-fund ministerial-level International Monetary and Financial Committee and the Development Committee, and the executive boards. The creation of the two "Camdessus councils" would constitute a significant shift in governance for the IMF and the World Bank, replacing the IMFC and the Development Committee, which are only advisory bodies, with new decision-making councils. What is left unanswered is which countries would constitute the Camdessus councils. The questions of who is in, who is out, and what criteria are used to decide the country composition of any international governance body are the key unresolved issues in global governance.

ROLE OF THE EXECUTIVE BOARDS. The executive boards of the World Bank and the IMF have been critically examined with respect to both their composition and their role. Some observers think that the boards delve too deeply into the details of IFI loans, policies, and operations and, as a consequence, "miss the forest for the trees." For example, a recent report on the World Bank proposed undertaking a review of executive board functions and responsibilities in the bank with a view to "how to make the Board more strategic, with an emphasis on its central task of setting objectives and holding management to account."[5] IMF historian James Boughton has expressed similar ideas regarding the executive board of the IMF. Executive board meetings might be held less often to reduce the intrusion of the boards into day-to-day operations of both the fund and the bank. As a result, the boards could better oversee bigger-picture strategic management of IFIs derived from guidance provided by ministers and heads of state, on one hand, and senior management, on the other. Meetings might also be held on occasion in developing countries. Expanded summits should survey the context of global challenges, which are multisectorial in nature—and of the responses to them, which also must be multisectorial and hence interinstitutional—and provide critical guidance on the relative roles of various international institutions in addressing those challenges. Ministers could then follow their guidance in the new councils and in their instructions to their executive directors on the boards of the IFIs.

VOTING RULES. Clearly, the voting rules in international institutions have implications for which reforms are accepted by member countries. Rules can safeguard the interests of those who are being asked to decrease their influence and of those who are being asked to assume more responsibility. Hence, a discussion of shares should be taken up in conjunction with a discussion of rules. In chapter 2, James Boughton suggests that the supermajority rule, which requires 85 percent of the vote in order to act on certain major issues (and thereby allows the United States to have an effective veto on those issues), could be abolished or modified. The Center for Global Development (CGD) report on the World Bank argued that "options should explore . . . the merits of applying double majorities on some decisions (that is, 50 percent of all votes plus 50 percent of all members)."[6] As in summits, countries with power do not want to loose decisive influence and countries seeking to gain power want to increase their influence to avoid being dragged into appearing to agree to something with which they disagree. Rules could safeguard the interests of both groups of countries.[7]

Summit Reform

The difficulty of achieving significant reforms within the individual international institutions leads inexorably to the conclusion that some exogenous forces need to be brought to bear on them or within them to break the current stalemate. But the fact is that the obsolete country composition of the G-8 summits is even more extreme than that of the IFIs and the UN Security Council. That creates both a significant challenge as well as promising opportunity to reshape the structure of the summits and to redefine their purview and mandate to become the stewards of the international system. It is a challenge because achieving summit reform itself will not be easy. It is an opportunity, since summit reform could potentially become the handmaiden of IFI and UN reform.

SUMMIT FORM. Summit form should follow function. In considering summit reform, it is helpful to have the discussion of the purpose, mission, and function of a summit precede the discussion of its country composition and form. There is a danger in separating the two topics in that the issue of who should be in and who should be out may become so absorbing that those debating the issue lose sight of the fact that membership decisions should be based in part on the nature of the task to be accomplished. A reinvigorated mandate for the summits is needed as much as a new membership.

SUMMIT FUNCTIONS. The Centre for Global Studies at the University of Victoria in British Columbia, along with the Centre for International Governance Innovation in Waterloo, organized a series of conferences that teed up the key global challenges for summits so that, in the event that a new summit group is formed, issues will already be prepared for consideration and action by a new, enlarged group of leaders.[8] One way to think about the issues driving summit reform is to consider the extent to which urgent issues, such as infectious diseases or energy security, push the summit reform agenda forward because of the need to include additional countries beyond the G-8. Another is to consider to what extent the implementation of the Millennium Declaration and the Millennium Development Goals (MDGs), both derived from the UN Millennium General Assembly in September 2000 in New York, constitute a compelling agenda for summits. Still another is to consider the degree to which the economic and financial challenges facing the global economy in themselves require summit leadership.

Global health is not only urgent but also bedeviled by problems that health ministers and the World Health Organization (WHO) have not been able to deal with. A lot of money is earmarked for disease eradication, but virtually no WHO money and scant resources elsewhere are set aside to deal with the central health challenge in developing countries, namely strengthening public health systems. The poverty-development-health interfaces, implicit in the MDGs, lack the institutional and strategic force necessary to fix the fragmentation of the global health governance system (see chapter 7 by Waldman), which only summit-level leadership can provide. In addition, the world faces serious threats from global climate change and other environmental challenges. Some countries and leaders have recognized that, others have not. A leadership forum is needed in which the greatest number of the countries causing the greatest environmental threats and holding the key to their effective resolution can join in a search for a common understanding and approach. Such a forum currently does not exist; as in the health area, the global environmental architecture seems hopelessly fragmented (see chapter 8). Finally, security issues—proliferation of nuclear weapons, terrorism, drugs, transnational crime, small-arms trafficking—would also seem to require action by leaders at the highest level from a greater variety of countries. The UN and the concerned UN agencies currently are unable to provide the leadership forum at the apex needed to debate and address these issues effectively.

ALTERNATIVE SUMMIT OPTIONS. While "form follows function" is the right principle, no clear answers regarding the size and composition of an expanded summit grouping have emerged. One therefore can reasonably focus on alternative summit reform options that already are under discussion and evaluate them in relation to the criteria of representativeness, effectiveness, and political feasibility. Former Canadian prime minister Paul Martin is on record in *Foreign Affairs* and elsewhere in favor of ratcheting up the G-20 finance ministers group, which consists of ten industrial and ten big emerging market economies, to an "L-20" leaders-level summit group. Alternatives to that proposal include

—increasing the number of representatives of the poorest counties[9]

—using regional leaders as representatives at the global level, for example, by drawing on heads of state who rotate as leader of regional institutions such as the African Union, the Association of South East Asian Nations (ASEAN), the Commonwealth of Independent States (CIS), and others[10]

—adding the four most obvious candidates to the G-8 (that is, China, India, Brazil, and South Africa) to constitute a "core" L-12, which in turn could be augmented on a revolving basis by adding six to eight seats for different countries depending on the issue under consideration (a system known as "variable geometry")[11]

—collapsing the European seats in the G-8 into one chair in the G-20, thereby reducing the G-20 to a G-16, which could then be elevated to an L-16.[12]

Each of these options contains implicit trade-offs and compromises with respect to group size, representativeness, and effectiveness. Since legitimacy rests equally on inclusion and performance, there are tensions between these conflicting requirements that cannot be easily resolved but must be brokered. Discussing alternative options reveals the compromises that are necessary.

Do the Pieces Add Up?

Once the specific elements at play in both individual institutional reform and in summit reform are considered, the question that remains is whether there is a way of framing a package of issues that provides the opportunity for striking a "grand bargain" in which actions could occur on multiple fronts simultaneously, reinforcing each other. If a grand bargain could be struck, it might be possible to move forward from stalemate toward an international system that is more able to meet global challenges through more democratic, inclusive, and effective global governance.

Even if most observers might conclude that the potential for a grand bargain is small, actions in some specific areas may still be feasible. Such actions could be executed one by one without the creation of a framework for more dramatic systemic reform. But there could also be unexpected synergies and cross-cutting effects. For example, reform efforts in the IFIs that seek to enhance the role of emerging market economies and other important nonindustrial countries in IFI governance have made it clear that the G-8 also needs to be reformed. And then there are issues, such as global health and global environmental governance, that we believe are impossible to advance unless summit reform occurs first. Using summits as a vehicle for addressing these pressing issues might itself require the participation of countries beyond the G-8 which would bring about summit reform as a consequence. Whichever way the force field runs—whether institutional reform drives summit reform or vice versa—it is clear that international institutional reform and summit reform depend on each other. That fact illustrates the degree to which the international governance system is in crisis and requires actions on multiple fronts to enable it to adequately address the challenges of our times.

Notes

1. Edwin M. Truman, "Overview on IMF Reform," "Rearranging IMF Chairs and Shares: The Sine Qua Non of IMF Reform," and "An IMF Reform Package," in *Reforming the IMF for the Twenty-First Century*, edited by Edwin M. Truman (Washington: Institute for International Economics, 2006), pp. 31–126, 201–32, and 527–40.

2. Ralph C. Bryant, *Crisis Prevention and Prosperity Management for the World Economy* (Brookings, 2004).

3. "Double majority" means that any decision has to be approved by a majority of member countries as well as by a majority of members' shares in the institution. This approach gives smaller and poorer members a clearer and more effective role than does a single-majority voting approach based on members' economic weight or financial contributions.

4. Michel Camdessus, "International Financial Institutions: Dealing with New Global Challenges," Per Jacobsson Lecture, Washington, September 25, 2005 (www.perjacobsson.org/lectures.htm).

5. Center for Global Development, "The Hardest Job in the World: Five Crucial Tasks for the New President of the World Bank," CGD Working Group Report, in *Rescuing the World Bank: A CGD Working Group Report and Selected Essays*, edited by Nancy Birdsall (Washington: Center for Global Development, 2006)

6. Ibid., p. 27.

7. Colin I. Bradford Jr., "Global Governance for the Twenty-First Century," Brookings, 2005, p. 15.

8. Centre for Global Studies (www.global centres.org).

9. Gerry Helleiner, "Leaders and Letters," *Financial Times*, January 4, 2006.

10. Martin Albrow and Colin I. Bradford Jr., "Regionalism in Global Governance: Realigning Goals and Leadership with Cultures," in *Regionalisation and the Taming of Globalisation?* edited by Andrew F. Cooper, Christopher Hughes, and Philippe de Lombaerde (London: Routledge, forthcoming, 2007).

11. Bradford, "Global Governance for the Twenty-First Century."

12. Fred C. Bergsten, "A New Steering Committee for the World Economy," in *Reforming the IMF for the Twenty-First Century,* edited by Edwin M. Truman (Washington: Institute for International Economics, 2006), pp. 279–92.

PART I

International Institutional Reform

1

IMF Reform:
Congruence with Global
Governance Reform

JACK BOORMAN

A reassessment of the mechanisms of global governance and proposals for institutional reform, including reform of the International Monetary Fund (IMF), are high on the agenda of the international community. A number of aspects of global governance that involve the IMF are included in the IMF managing director's medium-term strategy, which was discussed at the spring 2006 meeting of the International Monetary and Financial Committee (IMFC). On the matter of quotas and representation—a long-standing source of tension in the community—the managing director proposed a two-step process. In the first stage, by the time of the annual meetings in Singapore in September 2006, ad hoc increases in quotas would be agreed on in order to rectify the underrepresentation of member countries whose quota shares were seen as being most egregiously out of line with their place in the world economy. Those countries would likely include China, Korea, Mexico, Turkey, and possibly some others.[1] The proposed increases are intended, among other things, to halt the perceived drift away from the IMF of some members, especially in Asia, that do not have the voice in the institution that their economic and financial position in the global economy warrants.

The views expressed in this chapter are those of the author and not necessarily those of the International Monetary Fund or its management

But the increase in quotas is to be only the beginning. In the second stage, even more fundamental issues would be taken on, including

—the possibly less obvious misalignments of country quotas

—the construct of the quota formulas themselves

—the matter of what is called "basic votes," that is, the minimum number of votes assigned to every IMF member[2]

—the very tricky questions of representation on the IMF executive board. In that context, the issues could include deeper questions about the size of the board; whether the board should be resident at the IMF, as it has always been, or should be nonresident, as Keynes initially proposed; and perhaps even the seniority of officials appointed or elected to the board.

Officials attending the spring 2006 IMFC meeting agreed that ad hoc quota increases should be considered in Singapore, but only in the context of somewhat more specific proposals regarding how the more fundamental issues might be addressed. As John Snow said in his remarks to the IMFC: "The United States can only support a limited ad hoc quota increase in Singapore if it is credibly linked as a down payment on near-term fundamental reform."[3] Other members have similar views.

There is, of course, another layer of issues that involve IMF governing bodies besides the executive board, including the IMFC, the twenty-four-member ministerial body that represents the same constituencies as those represented on the executive board, and the board of governors, the body comprising ministers from each of the IMF's 184 member countries and the body from which the powers of the other governing bodies derive. While those two bodies have direct and formal responsibility for running the IMF, reflections on the governance of the fund must go well beyond the role played by those bodies. Because of the way that the global economic and financial system has been organized in the official sector, the IMF's formal governance structure is only one element of the much broader structure involving the agenda-setting and guiding bodies of the international economic and financial community. Those bodies include the G-7/8, the G-20, the G-24, the G-77, and others and the structures surrounding each of them: the deputies and the various technical working groups, below the ministerial level, and the summits or meetings of leaders, above the ministerial level.[4]

The IMF's formal governance structure has evolved through a somewhat ad hoc and not fundamentally democratic process and not necessarily according to any well-established and widely agreed-on set of principles. But suppose that the international community was starting over and had a blank slate with respect to that structure. What kind of system might it try to create? Here, let me echo a pessimistic note sounded some months ago by Martin Wolf in talking about the IMF. He recalls the oft-repeated phrase—at least by the fund's supporters—that if the IMF did not exist, it would have to be created. But in today's environment, he says, that would not happen. "We would not reinvent the Fund, not because it is useless," he said, "but because today's world lacks the courage and vision to create powerful multilateral institutions."[5] Indeed, today's world is one in which nations, or at least some of the major nations, seem unwilling to cede any of their sovereignty to international organizations.

Principles for Governance Reform

That difficult, but hopefully temporary, reality notwithstanding, is it possible to come up with a set of principles to guide the development of better governance structures—both of the IMF itself and its visible and formal governing bodies and of the broader agenda-setting and guiding bodies of the international economic and financial system, that is, the "Gs"? Some such principles are implicit, or even explicit, in the writings of others on the subject. But can a reasonably inclusive list of such principles be enumerated? This chapter attempts to create such a list and then asks how the current system stacks up against those principles, giving some concrete examples of what might be considered its failures or shortcomings. The chapter also suggests some actions that could be taken to make the system more faithful to those principles.

The suggested principles, which may tend to intersect and overlap, include the following:
—universality
—legitimacy, or what might be considered simple fairness
—subsidiarity
—efficiency
—accountability.
There also are a number of operational considerations—less like principles and more like practical guidelines—that also are important. They include
—capacity
—relevance
—informality, congeniality, and respect.

Universality

In a globalized world, the actions of one country—indeed, of individuals in one country—can affect every other country and the individuals therein, whether the actions involve economic activity, the environment, water use, public health, or a host of other areas. In such a world, every country should have some voice in global forums, both political and economic. That by no means implies that all forums must be global, open to participation by all countries. There is an important role for regional and other less-than-universal institutions and country groupings. But in a globalized world, there should be mechanisms to allow the forums that are more local to have a voice in the universal or global forums. The subsidiarity principle also argues for such a structure.

How does the IMF, charged in article I of its Articles of Agreement with promoting international monetary cooperation and financial stability, measure up under the principle of universality? Since the fall of the Soviet Union, the Fund has come very close to achieving universal membership.[6] But there is a difficult issue here. While virtually all countries belong to the IMF, the voice and vote of member countries vary widely. Similarly, the relationship of members to the institution and to each other is different from what was envisioned under the fund's original credit union–like character. Those relationships have changed dramatically with the expansion of the membership and with the growth of the private capital markets and the differential access of member countries to those markets.

In the original conception and with the original membership, it was anticipated that the financial resources of the IMF would revolve, or circulate, among the members—each country at times being a creditor and at other times a debtor. For some time now, however, the membership has tended to fragment into two groups of countries—some that are almost permanent creditors, and others that are either frequent or even permanent debtors. Thus, what was closer to a community of peers has become much less so. As an aside, the forecasts of some observers that this state of affairs will change as the Fund finds fewer debtors and ceases to be much of a lender should not be taken too seriously. Mervyn King, for example, in a widely reported speech in New Delhi in February 2006, said that "the growth of private capital flows and the build-up of massive foreign exchange reserves by many Asian economies have made redundant the idea that the primary function of the Fund is to be an international lender of last resort."[7] Others have expressed similar views. I agree with the view that the IMF's primary role should not be that of lender; it should be surveillance. And that role is clearly recognized in the second amendment to the fund's Articles of Agreement. But announcing the death of financial crises, or the end of a financing role for the fund in such crises, may be premature—not least because of the conditions that it can request of a borrowing country. The current benign economic and financial environment will not last and will be seen to have been a temporary lull in fund lending activity, as has often been the case in the past. The IMF will continue to have an important role to play as a lender in the inevitable future crises.

Thus, while the IMF is very close to being an all-inclusive organization, there is a question as to whether a genuine "commonality of interests" exists among its members. On one level, the answer certainly is yes. All countries have an interest in the primary mandate of the IMF—that is, to promote global economic and financial stability. But that commonality sometimes fades on issues specific to the policies and operations of the fund, such as access to its resources, the kind of conditions attached thereto, and other matters on which the creditors and the debtors sometimes part company in rather fundamental ways.

Even on something as basic as the IMF's primary responsibility—that is, surveillance of member country policies—the distinctions among members have an impact. The fund's influence over the policies of individual member countries is sometimes criticized as asymmetric: the IMF exercises more power and influence over the policies of member countries that periodically seek financing directly from the fund or from creditors or donors who may be influenced by the fund's views on those countries' policies; it exercises less influence over the policies of major creditor members, essentially the industrial countries. That critique has merit, and the IMF managing director's strategic review offers some suggestions with regard to it. Through the creation of new mechanisms of multilateral surveillance, the impact of surveillance—not least surveillance of the major shareholder countries—could be strengthened. In addition, through efforts to increase the voice and vote of those members that are currently seen to be underrepresented—some of whom are, or recently have been, borrowers—a better balance of power may be struck between creditor and debtor members.

The IMFC has endorsed a new framework for multilateral surveillance and has asked for concrete proposals to improve the distribution of quotas. What will come of this is unclear. John Snow, at the IMFC, supported the proposed multilateral consultations but with the caveat that "they are small, informal, and take place at senior management levels."[8] That view is probably realistic, but if they are only that, can they, at the same time, satisfy the objective of universality? It is hoped that effective modalities for multilateral consultations will be designed and some of them will succeed, helping to preserve both the universality of the institution and its substance—that is, the commonality of interests of its members.

Going beyond the formal structure of IMF governance to the broader structure of the global governance system through which countries also influence the fund, the picture is even more complicated. The G-7 and even the G-20 are hardly universal, although the latter comes much closer to something like the ideal than the former. And, of course, there are fundamental questions about the legitimacy and effectiveness of these groups. Moreover, although there are multiple regional forums, it is not clear that they build in a coherent fashion to a system that facilitates effective representation within the G-7 or the G-20 groupings. In fact, the multiplicity of such forums may well be one of the factors limiting their impact. What is needed are more effective vehicles through which the views put forward and the positions taken in regional and other forums can effectively percolate up to the predominant forums—today, the G-7/8. The international community needs to think in terms of what might be called a "ladder of representation" that can ensure that a channel exists whereby the views of the many can find some voice at the top. That takes us to the next principle.

Legitimacy

Under the principle of legitimacy, some concept of "fairness" in representation should be included. To a certain extent, any definition of "fairness" is and must be a matter of perception because there are no hard and universally accepted criteria to determine whether something is legitimate and fair. The dictionary is of little help here! Webster defines "legitimacy" as "accordant with law or with established legal forms and requirements" and as "conforming to recognized principles or accepted rules and standards." But the first of these is a bit circular: who establishes the "legal forms and requirements" and how are they established? Neither of the suggested meanings is operationally very meaningful. Carlo Cottarelli, in an interesting IMF working paper, says that "legitimacy means that its [an official organization's] actions must be seen as expressing an accepted source of power delegated to it by sovereign countries."[9] But there are problems with the absence of specific rules governing how that power is delegated. What or who is it that grants the right to representation and determines the nature and extent of that representation? Is it military power? Economic might? Population size? There is, quite obviously, no agreement in today's world on the answer to that question.

Perhaps the dictionary is more helpful in defining "fairness," inter alia, as "achieving a proper balance of conflicting interests." In the end, the members of a group—for example, the members of the IMF—must feel that they are fairly represented; that is, that they are represented in a way that helps achieve a reasonable balance of their conflicting interests. But does that feeling exist when, at the global governance level, as Leo Van Houtven, the former secretary of the IMF, puts it, "the major industrial countries, the G-7 . . . have exhibited a growing tendency in recent years to act as a self-appointed steering group or 'Directoire' of the IMF."[10] That tendency, together with the slow pace at which the IMF has adjusted the representation of members as their place in the world economy has changed, has had a harmful effect on the tradition of consensus building and therefore on members' sense of fairness and of ownership in the fund.

The governing structure of the IMF should provide legitimacy, and it should be seen as legitimate by its members as well as by people outside the institution. Perhaps the question can be put as follows: what governance features of an organization make sovereign countries find it acceptable to work with the organization and give up some of their sovereign power in doing so—and make that ceding of sovereignty acceptable to their populations? Suppose the IMF is put to that test. Representation in the IMF is determined primarily by the quota granted to a member country, and quotas are based on a formulaic effort to measure the role of the country in the global economic and financial system. The basic variables included in the formulas are GDP (at market exchange rates); openness (as measured by current receipts and payments); variability (meaning vulnerability to balance-of-payment shocks); and holdings of international reserves.

But many observers think that the current formulas need to be revisited, not least because they question the legitimacy of the representative structure that results from the formulas. Suggestions include changing the weight or the measurement of some of the variables already included or perhaps including new variables. For example, some suggest using a purchasing power parity (PPP) measure of GDP; others, including Michel Camdessus, a former IMF managing director, would include population. But this important issue remains unresolved, and even if the concepts of legitimacy and fairness cannot be given precise operational meaning, it is perfectly clear that some of the current quotas in the fund are perceived by many as illegitimate or unfair.

The basis for that perception is easy to see. A great deal of material is available on the anomalies of current quotas.[11] By way of example, the aggregate quota of the twelve Eurozone countries is 23.3 percent of total quotas;

for the twenty-five countries in the European Union (EU 25) together, it is 32.2 percent of total quotas. The share for the United States is 17.4 percent. Neither the EU nor the Eurozone constitutes a country in the same sense that the United States does, but as monetary policy, trade policy, and other financial and economic authority is transferred to Brussels and to Frankfurt from the member states, the more similar the two entities begin to look. If one thinks of what the U.S. quota would be if trade among the fifty states were included in the U.S. measure of current payments and receipts, it certainly raises questions about the inclusion of intercountry trade in the quota calculations for Europe. As another example, if one looks at the quotas of some of the larger emerging market countries—such as China, Korea, Mexico, Turkey, and others—large discrepancies are seen when comparing their quotas with those of other countries, including many in Europe, that have a much smaller role in the world economy. Korea, for example, with three times the output of Denmark, has a smaller quota in the IMF.

Beyond the issue of quotas is, of course, the matter of voice within the fund. To a great extent, that is a function of representation on the executive board. But again, there are some questionable realities. Of the EU 25 countries, three appoint their own executive director; other EU 25 countries are represented in no fewer than six additional multicountry constituencies, generally holding the position of executive director. These realities are important because if changes are to occur in quota shares, there will have to be some reduction in European shares; similarly, if representation on the executive board is to change or the size of the board is to decrease, it is difficult to see how such changes can come about without a reduction in the number of executive directors appointed or elected by the European countries.

The voices of the countries most affected by the IMF's policies also need to be reconsidered in making any changes. That could be dealt with both by changing the number of basic votes that each country is granted—moving the fund back to something closer to the original conception of the purpose of basic votes—and by looking at the capacity of countries to represent themselves effectively.[12]

Subsidiarity

There is a well-accepted view in the theory of social organizations that functions that subordinate organizations perform effectively belong more properly to them than to a dominant central organization. That is, in some ways, a "voice" issue, in that one leaves specific policies and decisions to those most affected by them but within a broad framework established by the more dominant or global organization. Leaving issues to those likely to have the greatest expertise would also generally support the principle of subsidiarity. This principle also helps to limit the agenda of the more global organization or authority, hopefully producing greater efficiency.

Basically, the subsidiarity principle says that issues ought to be settled as close to the ground as possible, but within an overall framework agreed on at the more global level. This is not an easy matter to resolve. In the political realm in the United States, for example, it involves the issue of states' rights and the uneasy balance maintained between power at the federal level to set overarching policies and power at the state and local levels to implement policies.

When thinking about optimal arrangements at the global level, one should ask whether there has been a tendency to pull issues unnecessarily—and perhaps at times counterproductively—to the top, to ministers or even to summits, rather than dealing with them in the relevant lower-level institutions. Surely guidance from the top is necessary and can be helpful, not least of all in order to know what is acceptable at the political level. But if issues are taken to too great a level of detail or specificity at the top, that can not only waste time and effort but also cause problems in the implementing institutions and resentment among members that were excluded from the top-level deliberations. A case can be made that this was a problem in some of the discussions regarding the reform of the international financial architecture in the aftermath of the financial crises of the 1990s. Some may remember the extraordinarily detailed annexes to the G-7 finance ministers' communiqués of that era. More recently, this issue arose in the formulation of the multilateral debt reduction initiative (MDRI) to grant 100 percent debt relief to some of the world's poorest countries. In that case, the initial proposals formulated by the G-7 deputies and agreed to by the ministers and leaders ran afoul of the IMF's Articles of Agreement, under which all members are bound, and the proposals had to be reformulated in the institutions. Greater involvement and attention at a subordinate level and within the relevant institutions—primarily the IMF and the World Bank in the case of the MDRI—could have avoided that outcome.

Efficiency

Cottarelli has examined the trade-offs between efficiency and governance in the IMF. Among other things, he points to the implications that the search for efficiency can have in an organization like the fund for the distribution of power between the "political pole," that is, the shareholders, and the "technocratic pole," that is, management and staff. Greater delegation generally enhances efficiency, but it can have significant implications for the way in which the various parties exert their influence. Of course, ultimate responsibility for the way that the IMF is run and for the decisions that it takes rests with the sovereign governments that are its members. I will come back to this point.

The more practical efficiency issues involving the fund that are currently on the table include the size and organization of the executive board and, by implication, the size of the IMFC. At the global level, these questions involve the size and composition of the global agenda-setting and guiding bodies—the "Gs." Let me say something only about the executive board. A couple of things need careful consideration.

First is the size of the board. There is fairly broad agreement that it is too large to operate efficiently—perhaps even effectively. Second is the seniority of directors within their own governments. There is quite a mix among directors in that regard, but generally speaking, it would be better if the level of seniority was raised; doing so might also help increase the independence of directors. That proposal adds a complication, however, in that such a change may be possible only if the board is made nonresident, with more-senior officials coming to Washington only periodically, perhaps monthly, to provide the oversight required and to consider the major policy, country-related, and administrative decisions that need to be taken.

Second is a matter of process. A practice has developed in the board whereby executive directors may submit a written statement on an agenda item ahead of a meeting. That was initiated primarily as a means of shortening meetings by setting down some of the more routine elements of an agenda item that an executive director wanted to include in the minutes and as a means of establishing positions, to the extent possible, ahead of the meeting. Most directors now submit such statements for most board meetings involving policy issues. It seems, however, that the possible gain in efficiency is now severely outweighed by the cost in terms of dialogue, discussion, and the search for consensus—something critical to the operation of the IMF. The room for maneuver of most executive directors may be reduced once positions are set down in black and white, especially if those positions have been vetted and agreed to by capitals. Board meetings must be an opportunity to learn something new, to see things from different perspectives, and, as a result, at times to modify positions. Current practice seems to operate against that.

Accountability

In any organization, accountability needs to be clear. But where and with whom does accountability lie in the IMF? And where does it lie within the agenda-setting bodies at the global level?

Given the way that the IMF is supposed to be managed, accountability should, in the first instance, rest with the managing director. But under the Articles of Agreement, the managing director is to carry out the business of the fund "subject to the general control of the Executive Board."[13] However, it is at least worth asking whether the board has developed practices and procedures that allow it to exercise oversight and control effectively and to the extent required—but without micromanaging in a way that makes it more difficult to hold management and senior staff accountable for their decisions.

On the highest level, it is of course the sovereign governments of the member countries that bear ultimate responsibility for the IMF and its decisions. But are they seen as accountable? There was a telling statement in a speech by Michel Camdessus to the Council on Foreign Relations in February 2000, around the time of his departure from the IMF. Speaking on this issue, he said: "The problem is not that we are not accountable, but that we are not seen to be accountable, and that some member governments from time to time find it convenient not to express their public support for actions they have supported in the Executive Board."[14] I believe that his remark was a candid expression of the frustration that he felt with the fact that some governments seemed publicly to be second-guessing or even distancing themselves from some of the controversial operations of the fund, especially in Russia and in some of the Asian crisis countries. He went on to say that "it is . . . important to insure that the IMF is seen far more visibly to have legitimate political support of our shareholders." To that end, he proposed transforming the IMF's advisory ministerial committee (today's IMFC) into a decisionmaking council for the major strategic operations facing the fund. As he said, "This would simply, in the eyes of the public, place responsibility squarely where it already exists." He expanded the proposal in a speech in September 2005, saying that "the Council . . . would be the ideal place to discuss the policies needed to address global systemic issues with a global membership, and thus to take the place also of the G10, G20 and other Gs."[15] He seemed to imply that he would retain the G-7.

Thus far Camdessus has not persuaded the community to create the council. He did succeed in transforming the Interim Committee into the current IMFC in September 1999, a significant step toward creating a permanent body. However, the IMFC is still only an "advisory" and not a decisionmaking body. More recently, Peter Kenen has taken up the proposal to form a council, but in the context of a broader set of changes to the executive board and to the voting power of participants in the council and in the executive board.[16] These ideas deserve a full debate in the context of the principles elaborated above.

The issue of accountability, as evident in Camdessus's recent reiteration of his proposal to create a decisionmaking council, cannot be discussed without bringing in the role played by the Gs, especially the G-7/8 and the G-20 and, perhaps to a lesser extent, the G-10, whose role has faded in the last years. It is in those forums that many issues are deliberated and debated and positions determined. Those issues may then be brought into the IMF, but only after a certain level of agreement has been reached among the participants in the forums. It should be clear that good ideas should be accepted from any source and any forum. But two issues within the current system call for reflection. The first is the balance that must be struck, under the principle of universality, between raising and formulating ideas in the G-1, G-3, G-7, or elsewhere and the need—indeed requirement, if real meaning is to be given to the participation and involvement of others—for consultation with the rest of the community in deciding the final outcome of a debate or in taking decisions on an issue. It weakens members' sense of ownership and challenges the concepts of universality and legitimacy when the G-7, for example, brings an idea into the IMF that has been too finely tuned and cannot be subject to genuine debate and modification. In the end, such a practice also blurs the issue of accountability: does it lie with the universal membership of the fund or with the smaller groups? Such has been the case on a number of important policy issues and in a number of critical country operations.

The second issue involves the breach of the subsidiarity principle that occurs when the G-7 or another forum takes an issue that the community may be disposed to support to a level of detail and specificity that precludes genuine discussion, debate, and consensus building or makes them very difficult. Sometimes that seems to occur because concessions must be made to find agreement within the G-7, but the balance then struck makes later modification in the IMF and elsewhere much more difficult. This issue involves a difficult trade-off. But the objective should be to frame issues in the smaller groups in more general terms, sufficient to secure the political agreement needed to move them forward, and then to bring those issues into the IMF or other relevant institutions in a manner that permits genuine debate and reformulation and, it is hoped, wider consensus on—and ownership of—the outcome. Formulating the specifics of an issue closer to the ground within the affected institution will almost always result in better and more widely owned and accepted policies.

Other Issues

Finally, there are a few other considerations that should guide governing bodies, both those of the IMF and other international institutions and those of the agenda-setting groups.

Countries must have the talent and capacity to represent themselves effectively, and institutions must have sufficient staff—in terms of numbers and of skills—to do the job requested of them. With regard to country representation, most of the responsibility, of course, rests with the country itself to find the needed talent. But that is not always easy to do given the competing demands within government for what is, in many cases, a limited talent pool, especially in low-income countries. Beyond that—and in the context of the IMF—there must be sufficiently experienced personnel available to staff the offices of the executive directors and similar offices. Here, I believe, the IMF falls short, even though there have been efforts in the recent past to improve the situation. For example, the two IMF executive directors who represent most of Africa have nineteen and twenty-four countries, respectively, in their constituencies. Of those forty-three countries, a large majority have financial arrangements with the IMF or are in discussions or negotiations toward entering such an arrangement. Managing the relationship between the IMF and a country that has a financial arrangement with the fund is a time-consuming and difficult activity. But the two executive directors mentioned have only a very few more positions in their offices than the other directors have. The result is less effective representation and less intense involvement in the policy issues and important country matters confronting the institution. That weakens the voice of the countries involved on matters that affect the IMF itself and the global economy and on policies that determine the operational framework of the fund with constituent countries. That was painfully evident in the formulation of the Heavily Indebted Poor Countries (HIPC) Initiative. If the board is reconfigured, this issue should also be addressed.

Relevance means ensuring that the right people are around the table when an issue is being discussed; those would be people representing the governments with the greatest stake in the issue. Perhaps the most anomalous example in recent years has been the discussions of the Chinese current account surplus and the value of the renminbi that have taken place in the G-7/8. At times, the Chinese have been invited in, but that is a distant second-best to having a forum that includes all relevant parties as full and active participants. As Peter Kenen, Nigel Wicks, Jeff Shafer, and Charles Wyplosz proposed, the topic would probably be dealt with best in a G-4 comprising the United States, China, Japan, and a Eurozone representative.[17] On a broader level, the proper forum for such a discussion is the IMF executive board, in the first instance, and the IMFC or, perhaps, Camdessus's proposed IMF decisionmaking council. All countries have a stake in the configuration of the major currencies and should have the opportunity to have their views heard in a proper forum. That does not mean that the final policy agreements could be worked out in that forum; doing so requires a high degree of confidentiality on an issue as sensitive as the major exchange rates. But somewhere in the process, the voices of those that may be significantly affected by such agreements should be heard. What roles will emerge for the IMF executive board and the IMFC is a key negotiating point in the IMF reform effort currently under discussion by member governments. Achieving closure on key points will not be easy, given the apparent differences of views among some of the major participants.

Finally, informality, congeniality, and respect should be characteristics of any gathering in the international community.

Current Reform Prospects

So where does this take us? The IMF managing director's medium-term strategy addresses many of the issues raised above and has received the IMFC's endorsement. Generally speaking, the strategy hits most of the right notes in trying to accommodate the principles listed above. With respect to specific points:

First, the proposed multilateral consultations could go some distance toward bringing the major problems now confronting the global economy and financial system—such as the global current account imbalances—into the forum in which they belong, the IMF.

Second, the proposal to extend the analyses of equilibrium exchange rates and to find some way to bring greater transparency to the process and to the conclusions would help to put the IMF closer to the center of the discussions on these issues.

Third, the proposed ad hoc quota increases and subsequent, more fundamental, review of the quota formulas, basic votes, and related issues have the potential to significantly improve the IMF's real and perceived legitimacy and members' interest—and sense of ownership—in the IMF. Reconsidering Camdessus's proposal to replace the IMFC with a decisionmaking council and opening up the question of the size and composition of the executive board would take this process one important step further. So, too, would progress on the managing director's statement that "a transparent procedure for the selection of the Managing Director should be formally approved." The selection process for the first deputy managing director should be added to that agenda.

Fourth, reopening issues such as the IMF's policy on lending into arrears and reconsidering the Contingent Credit Line (CCL) or some other kind of insurance mechanism for emerging market members could go some way toward renewing the emerging market countries' interest in the IMF. Here, however, the prospects seem uncertain; as John Snow said in his remarks to the IMFC in April 2006, the United States "remain[s] unconvinced that the proposed new instruments to support emerging markets are necessary and appropriate."[18]

There will be many devils in the details when efforts are made to elaborate on these proposals and make them more specific, let alone to decide when they should be implemented. Even though this is an ambitious package, still other suggestions could be incorporated. One that I would mention is clarification of the role of the IMF in the process of capital account liberalization by its members. There are a number of myths about the past role of the fund regarding this issue. Fortunately, some of those myths were nicely debunked by a review of its role that was conducted by the IMF's Independent Evaluation Office.[19] Perhaps the issue will resurface when the role and structure of the new department to be created out of the merger of the former International Capital Markets Department and the Monetary and Financial Systems Department are decided. This is an important issue in terms of clarifying the role of the IMF going forward.

With regard to the implications for the global agenda-setting bodies, I would offer only one additional thought. In considering the best configuration of countries within a global group, it would seem desirable to keep the overall pattern of regional groups and of the institutional governing bodies in mind. As already indicated, the regional groups should build in some coherent fashion—through a ladder of representation—up to the global group so that all parties in the regional groups feel that they have a channel to the dominant group. In addition, the global group itself should mirror in some comprehensive way the composition of the institutional governing bodies and vice versa. For example, if a group approximately the size of the G-20 is kept, it should be reformed in a way that makes it truly universal and mirrors the composition of the IMFC. In the event of more substantial reform, the G-20 could mirror or even be replaced by the proposed council.

Notes

1. At the September 2006 annual meetings, the IMF board of governors approved quota increases for China, Korea, Mexico, and Turkey as part of a package of IMF quota and voice reforms to be completed no later than by the 2008 annual meetings.

2. At the time of the creation of the IMF, each member was assigned 250 votes, cumulatively amounting to 11.3 percent of total votes in the fund. (A member has 250 basic votes regardless of the size of its quota and one vote per 100,000 special drawing rights of its quota.) That number of basic votes has never been changed, and as quotas increased over time, basic votes have declined to 0.021 percent of total votes. That decline obviously affects members with the smallest quotas most severely.

3. John W. Snow, "IMFC Statement by the Honorable John W. Snow, Secretary of the Treasury, United States of America," April 22, 2006, p. 3 (www.imf.org/external/spring/2006/imfc/index.asp [October 26, 2006]).

4. This note considers only the way in which the official community is organized to govern the international monetary and financial system. It leaves out considerations regarding the role of the private sector, both in working with the official sector and in influencing or participating in the governing structure. That is a separate topic, but as private capital flows have come to dominate financial flows, an increasingly important one.

5. Martin Wolf, "World Needs Independent Fund," *Financial Times*, February 21, 2006.

6. This was not the case for the first forty years or so of the IMF's existence because Stalin refused to ratify the Articles of Agreement, which had been signed ad referendum by the Soviet delegation to Bretton Woods.

7. Mervyn King, governor of the Bank of England, "Reform of the International Monetary Fund," speech given at the Indian Council for Research on International Economic Relations (ICRIER), New Delhi, India, February 20, 2006 (www.bankofengland.co.uk/publications/speeches/speaker.htm#king [October 26, 2006]).

8. Snow, "IMFC Statement."

9. Carlo Cottarelli, "Efficiency and Legitimacy: Trade-Offs in IMF Governance," IMF Working Paper WP/05/107 (Washington: International Monetary Fund), p. 3.

10. Leo Van Houtven, *Governance of the IMF: Decisionmaking, Institutional Oversight, Transparency, and Accountability* (Washington: International Monetary Fund, 2002).

11. See, for example, Ariel Buira, "The IMF at Sixty: An Unfilled Potential," in *The IMF and The World Bank at Sixty*, edited by Ariel Buira for the G-24 Research Program (London: Anthem Press, 2005).

12. Jim Boughton makes the interesting point that while a change in basic votes would require an amendment to the Articles of Agreement—probably unlikely in today's environment—the same result could be achieved by other means.

13. Articles of Agreement, article XII, section 4b.

14. "An Agenda for the IMF at the Start of the 21st Century: Remarks by Michel Camdessus at the Council on Foreign Relations," Council on Foreign Relations, New York, February 1, 2000.

15. Michel Camdessus, "International Financial Institutions: Dealing with New Global Challenges," Per Jacobssen Lecture, Washington, September 25, 2005 (www.perjacobssenlecture.org/lectures.htm).

16. Peter B. Kenen, remarks made at the Institute for International Economics, Washington, April 20, 2006.

17. Peter Kenen and others, "International Economic and Financial Cooperation: New Issues, New Actions, New Responses" (International Center for Monetary and Banking Studies, Geneva, and Center for Economic Policy Research, London, 2004).

18. Snow, "IMFC Statement."

19. "Report on the IMF's Approach to Capital Account Liberalization" (Washington: IMF Independent Evaluation Office, May 2005).

2

Strengthening the IMF: Lessons from History

JAMES M. BOUGHTON

The International Monetary Fund (IMF) was designed and founded at a strategically important moment in world history. The Allied victory in World War II was in sight, and the economic depression of the 1930s was still a vivid memory. Consequently, the collective will to avoid a repetition of the quarter century of chaos that had followed World War I spearheaded multilateral discussions on how to create a stable economic and financial system for the postwar world. In the ensuing six decades, despite the many problems associated with globalization, the success of that system has far exceeded the vision of the delegates at Bretton Woods in 1944. International trade and the globalization of finance, while far less stable than one might hope, have been the engine for spectacular growth in world output and living standards. For the twenty-five years through 2001, for example, world trade in real terms grew at an annual rate of 5.8 percent and world real GDP grew at a rate of 3.4 percent.[1]

I am grateful to Jack Boorman, Colin Bradford, Graham Hacche, Sean Hagan, and Russell Kincaid for comments on earlier drafts and to participants in seminars sponsored by the IMF, the Brookings Institution, the Global Interdependence Center, and the Centre for International Governance Innovation for helpful suggestions. The views expressed here are entirely personal and should not be interpreted as those of the IMF or other institutions.

As a corollary to this success, the world economy has changed markedly, and the IMF has had to adapt in many ways in order to maintain its effectiveness. Two changes have had especially dramatic effects on the IMF.

First, the structure of the membership of the IMF as a club of peers in which almost any member might be a creditor one year and a debtor the next has given way to divisions in which many representatives see themselves as more or less permanent members of a creditor or (potentially) indebted group. For the first decade of operations, from 1946 to 1955, the IMF had one creditor country: the United States. Canada became a creditor in 1956, and then the number gradually increased. Today the IMF has forty-six creditor countries—a quarter of the membership—including countries on every continent. For example, Botswana, even though it is located in the world's poorest region, sub-Saharan Africa, is a creditor of the IMF.

At the outset virtually all members other than the United States were likely to need to borrow from the IMF occasionally to settle their external balance of payments. Of the thirty-nine original members that paid in their quota subscriptions, all but two borrowed or drew on their subscriptions at least once during the first twenty-five years. Today, as a consequence of postwar global economic growth, twenty members have been creditors of the IMF since at least the end of the 1980s, and most of those and more seem unlikely to borrow in the future. Even though a large number of countries still swing from one camp to the other from time to time, states tend strongly to view themselves as members of a creditor group or a borrower group. The membership thereby has become more and more polarized, with the largest and most powerful countries mostly in the creditor group.[2]

Second, the role in international finance of private cross-border capital flows has mushroomed. In the immediate postwar era, trade flows were financed largely through official channels and trade credits. Today private capital flows that are not directly related to trade are a dominant influence on the financial health of many countries. As a result, the financial and governance structures of the IMF—which are based primarily on countries' economic size and the magnitude of their trade flows—may no longer correspond to the most relevant indicators of members' importance or need.

In response to these and other changes, in 2004 the managing director of the IMF initiated a "strategic review" of the institution to update the interpretation of its mandate, reexamine and revamp the tools available for fulfilling its mandate, and refocus operations on its updated priorities. Practical steps under active consideration as of mid-2006 include raising the quotas (and thus the voting shares) of countries that have experienced rapid economic growth in recent years, enhancing the IMF's role in multilateral policy discussions by introducing new procedures for multilateral surveillance, and enhancing the institution's ability to assess and report on departures from equilibrium exchange rates.[3]

This chapter steps back from the practical issues that are guiding the strategic review and looks more broadly at some principles to guide thinking about the longer-term future role of the IMF, drawing on the lessons that have emerged from postwar economic and financial history. How the world will change in the years to come is unknowable, but one may safely predict that change will continue and will in all likelihood be even more dramatic and rapid than in the past. The key to successful adaptation is not to reflect the world of today, but to anticipate the future and be flexible enough to respond to whatever changes are likely to occur in the next few decades.

These considerations suggest that a comprehensive strategy for adaptation and reform should include three main elements:

—strengthening and deepening the IMF's core competencies as a policy adviser to its members

—reunifying the institution's now somewhat fragmented role across the full range of its member countries

—modernizing the way that the institution is governed and making it more flexible.

Core Competencies

The initial element of any comprehensive strategy should be to ensure that the IMF continues to have the means to provide policy advice of the highest quality to the monetary authorities of its member countries. For two reasons, that ability could be endangered.

The first reason is that the IMF is an episodic lender. It does not lend steady or predictable amounts of money from one year to the next. Rather, it responds to both localized and more global shocks that enlarge international payments imbalances or reduce the willingness of markets to finance them. In a world of large and volatile private capital flows, when a major financial crisis occurs, the IMF may be called in by the affected countries to provide both loans and policy advice. The fund's policy expertise may be needed both directly, to help a country resolve the problems that contributed to the crisis in the first place, and indirectly, to restore the confidence of other creditors (private and official) whose financial support will be needed if recovery is to be sustained. For the IMF to play its role effectively, it must continuously

Figure 2-1. *IMF Lending, 1948–2005, Percent of World Imports*[a]

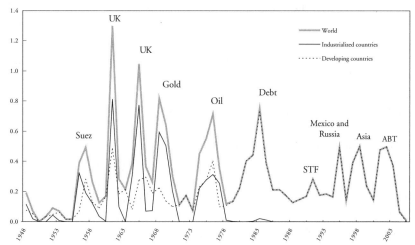

a. Labels indicate the main reason for the spike. UK = United Kingdom; STF = Systemic Transformation Facility; ABT = Argentina, Brazil, and Turkey.
Source: International Monetary Fund, "International Financial Statistics" (www.imf.org).

maintain the quality of its general and its country-specific expertise in order to be prepared to respond when the unpredictable occurs. The longer the world—or even a region or an individual country—goes without a crisis, the more challenging it is for the IMF to maintain the quality and readiness of its staff and the more important it is to maintain close relations with the monetary authorities in countries that might one day again need help.

How important to institutional readiness are the intervals between crises? Major financial crises have arisen with disturbing regularity for half a century now, and each one has produced a sharp spike in IMF lending followed by a lull of at least a few years. The pattern of the past decade, which seems so dramatic when viewed over the short term, is in fact not at all unusual in the broader sweep of history (figure 2-1). The potential for a serious institutional problem occurs only when the lull is prolonged, as it was at the very outset (for the decade preceding the 1956 Suez crisis) and to a much lesser extent in 1978–81 and the late 1980s. If the urgency of the fund's work dissipates over more than a few years, then governments and central banks may question its value and take its advice less seriously, the institution may have increasing trouble attracting and retaining staff of the quality that it will need when the next crisis hits, and its financial resources will fail to keep pace with growth in the world economy.

The core modern function of the IMF, both in periods of crisis and in the lending lulls when the world economy is performing well, is surveillance. If the fund performs that task well, it enhances global financial stability and helps prevent crises from developing. The key to minimizing the negative institutional consequences of the favorable lulls between crises is to ensure that surveillance discussions with members and multilateral surveillance activities such as those reported in the *World Economic Outlook* and the *Global Financial Stability Report* are focused and effective and are seen as valuable by member countries.

The second reason is that the nature of the policy advice required in a crisis has expanded over time because of the changing nature of the IMF's membership and the growth in private international capital flows. Both developments have led to a concentration in fund lending on "emerging markets": developing countries whose access to private capital is substantial at times but limited and uncertain at other times. To help avoid financial crises and manage them effectively when they do occur, an emerging market country must develop and maintain a market and institutional structure that instills confidence in investors. To provide effective advice to such countries, the IMF must develop an expertise in financial market analysis that is on a par with the expertise on macroeconomic policies that it developed in its early years. Only if the fund is an acknowledged leader in both fields can it maintain its edge and credibility and its readiness to respond appropriately when it is most needed.

The IMF has maintained its macroeconomic expertise in the wake of the many changes in theory and policy analysis since the 1940s.[4] It has proved that it can compete with the leading universities for the best international macroeconomists in the world and that it can deliver very high-quality analysis pretty consistently to all of its member countries. Attracting and retaining the best people in international finance is much harder, because more of the competition comes from private financial institutions with very deep pockets and because the IMF has not yet developed a reputation as a breeding ground for financial talent that is as strong as its reputation for macroeconomic expertise. The fund is now working to overcome its late start in this area, which is one of the key challenges identified in its strategic review.

A Unified Institutional Strategy

As the world has become more divided into groups of countries, the IMF's work for each group has taken a different focus. These groupings effectively slice the world horizontally into three strata by per capita income levels, although the differences among them are too complex to be fully captured by such stratification.

At the top of the pyramid are some thirty "advanced economies" with high average income and domestic savings or ready access to private international capital markets or both. The IMF provides ongoing policy advice to these countries through its surveillance activities, but the impact is usually limited. These members tend to see themselves as providers rather than receivers of both money and expertise.

A second group comprises about seventy-five middle-income developing countries and countries in transition toward a market economy. These countries do not normally need or want loans from the IMF, but they may have occasional demand for large-scale temporary financing to help manage and resolve a crisis. When called on, the IMF makes loans to these countries contingent on their agreement to adopt changes in a potentially wide variety of national economic policies.

The third and largest group comprises nearly eighty low-income countries. Many of them are in the early stages of economic and institutional development and may lack the administrative capacity to run a national economy effectively; therefore they have an ongoing need for detailed policy advice. Because the IMF does not have the resources or the mandate to offer long-term development finance, its financial role in low-income countries is limited to providing small-scale but possibly persistent financing for stabilization and reform.

Despite its specialized roles, the IMF is and must be a universal institution.[5] The world is dynamic, and that fact is of key relevance to the future of the IMF. If there are thirty advanced economies and seventy-five middle-income countries today, in fifteen or twenty years there may be fifty advanced and 100 middle-income countries, leaving only thirty to forty low-income countries instead of the nearly eighty today. To achieve that degree of progress requires a universal institution that is fully engaged in helping countries move up the ladder. When a country needs assistance with macroeconomic issues or access to international finance, the IMF is the institution that is best placed to provide it, regardless of the country's current income level or state of development.

A related point is that it is not helpful to think of countries in terms of their status as creditors or debtors within the IMF or other official agencies. As the Republic of Korea has demonstrated in the past decade, even advanced economies can face adverse circumstances, and borrowing from the

IMF can play an important part in their recovery. Several countries that have borrowed from the fund to support their transition to a market-based economy—including China, the Czech Republic, Estonia, and Russia—are no longer debtors at this time. More generally, in the past twenty-five years more than forty countries have gone from being a net financial contributor or debtor to being a debtor or contributor and then back again. Many others are neither creditors nor borrowers, and that number seems likely to rise as alternative sources of international finance continue to grow. The polarization of the IMF membership between the two camps is not an illusion, but it is more perceptual than real.

A more relevant and helpful way to think about the different demands that members may place on the IMF is to adopt an alternative, dynamic taxonomy that looks forward more and focuses on members' financial differences rather than on differences in their income levels.

PRE-EMERGENT ECONOMIES. In the new taxonomy, the low-income category would be replaced conceptually by a similar but probably somewhat larger group of "pre-emergent" economies. These are countries that, whatever their income level, have very little or no access to private capital inflows and that therefore are totally dependent on official support for financing their external payments deficits. Most of these countries also have low domestic saving rates and therefore cannot generate economic growth without running external deficits. Compared with bilateral and multilateral donors that provide longer-term development assistance, the IMF is of secondary importance to these countries. But "of secondary importance" does not mean "unimportant."

Pre-emergent economies need a strategy for moving up the development ladder. They need advice on how to marry macroeconomic stability with the fiscal requirements for economic development, including spending on health, education, and infrastructure. They need assistance in assessing their financial needs and in obtaining as much donor financing as they can properly absorb. The IMF responds to their needs by providing both advice and temporary financial assistance, and that response is more effective to the extent that it is embedded within a dynamic development strategy.

EMERGING MARKETS. Similarly, the middle-income category can be replaced by emerging markets. These sixty to seventy countries have at least some access to private capital most of the time but do not have the assurance that those inflows will continue in periods of crisis.[6] That vulnerability is evident now even when a crisis arises in a distant part of the world, as became clear in the late 1990s when a sudden stoppage in Thailand reverberated around East Asia, then in Russia, and eventually in Brazil. Compared with private capital markets, the IMF is of secondary importance to this group of countries also. Again, however, that it is of secondary importance does not mean that it is unimportant.

Although the specifics of the advice needed by emerging-market countries and by pre-emergent economies may differ, its basic nature does not. The economies and the financial systems of emerging markets need to be managed in order to sustain the confidence of private investors (both domestic and foreign) and thereby minimize the risk of financial crisis. That requires the same general strain of macroeconomic and financial market analysis that the IMF provides to all countries. If a crisis does occur, it may also require the availability of large-scale financial assistance on short notice, either directly from the fund or organized through its auspices. The assistance would generally be contingent on the adoption of corrective policies intended both to minimize the short-term output loss and to bring the economy back to a path to sustainable growth. The overarching strategy for both the advice and the financing should, as in other cases, be aimed at helping these countries develop beyond the status of an "emerging" market.

ADVANCED ECONOMIES. At the top of the ladder, a position defined by financial development rather than income, are the advanced economies that enjoy ready and reliable access to private capital markets and have no current or expected future need to draw on official financing from the IMF. The fund is—at best—of secondary importance to these countries, compared with their own multilateral groupings such as the G-7, the European Union (EU), and the Organization for Economic Cooperation and Development (OECD). Even for this group, however, "of secondary importance" does not necessarily mean "unimportant."

The IMF offers advanced economies valuable analysis of regional and global interactions and spillovers, of possibly adverse consequences of one country's policies and economic conditions for the rest of the world, and of the longer-run consequences of policy choices. It also can offer a strategy (and a mind-set) for helping all countries develop and grow in a stable and sustainable way that enhances global economic welfare. While there is no shortage of expertise on such issues in the advanced economies, a multilateral agency brings the pooled experience of all countries to the table and can analyze how that experience bears on the challenges faced by others. The IMF thus is able to provide policy advice, a global public good, in a more systematic way than is possible within a single national government.

Overall, what is required is for the IMF to think and act dynamically and universally, in order to help all of its member countries advance economically and financially. If it succeeds, then fewer and fewer countries will borrow from the fund, not because of resistance to the IMF as an outside agent of control or a symbol of weakened economic sovereignty but simply because the system will have worked.

Modern Governance

The third element for strengthening the IMF—in addition to strengthening its core competencies and unifying its institutional role across the membership—is to modernize its governance structure and increase its flexibility to respond continually as the world evolves. Some facets of a modernization strategy, including the need for a more open and transparent leadership selection process, already have generated a broad consensus on principle. Others, notably the revitalization of voting and quota shares, have generated more controversy.[7]

The current sharing of governance of the IMF is bound by inertia, because most quota increases have been spread proportionally among member countries, ad hoc adjustments have been fairly rare, and no quota has ever been reduced (quotas can be reduced only with the consent of the country concerned). For example, because the Republic of Korea joined the IMF in 1955, when it was still a low-income and pre-emergent economy, it was assigned a very low quota share (0.14 percent of the total), just below the share of the countries now known as Myanmar and Sri Lanka. Because the Korean economy has grown at rates well above the world average, the country has received above-average quota increases, but until 2006 the increases were much less than needed to keep pace. Consequently, Korea's quota share was just below the shares of Denmark and of Norway, even though its GDP and volume of international trade were some three times theirs.

Partial solutions to this inertia are easy to devise, through ad hoc quota adjustments for members whose shares are most out of line. A general solution, which would establish and maintain quota shares at the appropriate levels, is far more difficult to achieve, and not only because of resistance from the countries whose shares would decline. The fundamental difficulty is that no ideal distribution exists and even a partially optimal distribution will continue to change as the world economy changes. Specifically, there are two distinct gaps between actual and optimal quotas, and they cut in opposite directions.

First, there is a "power gap" between current quotas at any time and the current distribution of economic size and power. As of 2006, to close that gap would require raising the shares of a number of countries that have grown rapidly, which are especially concentrated in Asia, and reducing the shares of some European countries that have grown relatively slowly. It also would require raising the U.S. share and reducing that of sub-Saharan Africa.[8] Not surprisingly, it is easier to develop consensus on the shares to be raised than on those to be reduced as an offset.

Second, there is a "peerage gap" between actual voting power and a reasonably fair distribution of influence across the world. "Fair" in this context does not necessarily refer to Westphalian (one vote per state) or democratic (one vote per person) principles, neither of which has compelling relevance for an institution such as the IMF. The fund's financial structure rules out the former and its nature as a membership organization of states rather than individuals rules out the latter.

A more compelling interpretation of fairness in this context is to ensure that members that are heavily affected by the fund's policies and actions have an effective voice in determining its policies and actions. When a member state applies to borrow money from the IMF, it represents that it needs the money because of a balance of payments problem, and it agrees to implement a set of policies aimed at resolving that problem. If the country's monetary authorities or others in positions of power and influence in the country do not believe that their views are adequately represented at the IMF, then the country becomes a supplicant rather than a partner in the policy negotiations. The country may therefore be less likely to take ownership of the policy regime and less willing to carry it out. Fairness is needed not just for its own sake but for its practical consequences for the effectiveness of fund operations.

Closing the peerage gap again means raising the quota shares of a number of emerging-market countries, including the fast-growing Asian economies, and lowering those of advanced European countries. In contrast to the requirements for closing the power gap, however, it may also require lowering the U.S. share and raising the shares of African and other countries that are subject to IMF loan conditions.[9] In any event, it will not generally be possible to close both the power gap and the peerage gap, and even if it were possible, the dynamism of the world economy would soon open new gaps that would be difficult or impossible to close.

The lasting solution to the inherent weaknesses in IMF governance lies not in trying to close the gaps but in trying to minimize their adverse consequences. Since no ideal distribution of quotas or voting shares will ever be found, the fund needs to look for measures that could be taken to move toward the best distribution feasible at any given time and live with it. The remainder of the chapter sets out eight such steps, ranging from those that could be implemented fairly easily and in some cases already have been, to those that would require greater political consensus than so far has materialized.

DELINKING BORROWING LIMITS FROM QUOTAS. The IMF's current access limits specify that a member country may borrow, subject to fund policies, up to 100 percent of its quota in any twelve-month period and up to 300 percent in total. In most cases, actual access approved under standby and other arrangements is well below those ceilings, as the fund decides on the basis of each borrower's circumstances. In reacting to major crises, the IMF may also grant exceptional access, notably through the supplemental reserve facility, which was established in response to the Korean crisis in 1997.

The more the distribution of quotas departs from the distribution of stress on members' balance of payments, the more compelling the logic for overriding quotas as the principal determinant in case-by-case decisions on the appropriate level of access. Moving further in the direction of delinking borrowing from quotas would require only a policy decision by the IMF executive board.

DELINKING FINANCIAL CONTRIBUTIONS FROM QUOTAS. The lendable resources of the IMF come not from the whole membership in proportion to quotas but from the (currently) forty-six creditor countries in rough proportion to their quotas.[10] Thus, while the United States holds 17 percent of the voting power, it provides about one-fourth of the usable currencies in the fund's general resources account. Other creditors provide proportionally smaller amounts.

To the extent that quotas do not reflect the actual distribution of countries' financial strength, departures could be introduced from the proportionality rule. For special purposes, a larger number of governments or central banks have contributed amounts that are not related to quotas at all, through ad hoc contributions to accounts that are administered by the IMF and used to help finance certain IMF lending operations such as the Poverty Reduction and Growth Facility (PRGF) Trust (for concessional lending to low-income countries) and the Heavily Indebted Poor Countries (HIPC) Trust (for debt relief for heavily indebted low-income countries). Several countries (Japan and Saudi Arabia being the predominant examples) have occasionally made loans to the fund for other purposes.[11] These practices could be generalized further under existing IMF policies.

STRENGTHENING CONSENSUS BUILDING. As a general practice, the IMF has always tried to operate through consensus. The taking of votes is a fairly rare event for the executive board, for either country matters (lending decisions) or broader policy decisions. Instead, the secretary of the IMF normally gets a sense of the directors' views from their formal and informal remarks, and dissenting views may be reflected in a summary of the meeting known as the "summing up."

As the board has become more polarized between the major creditors and others, achieving consensus has become more difficult. Formal vote-taking remains rare, but the prevailing view expressed in the sense of a meeting is often that of a majority dominated by creditors. To reverse this trend would require a strong commitment to consensus building by both senior management (such as the chair of the board) and by the executive directors who are most often in the majority.

NARROWING THE SCOPE OF POLICY ADVICE. In a trend that began in the 1980s and accelerated in the 1990s, the IMF gradually expanded the reach of its policy advice and its lending conditions to encompass a fairly wide range of structural economic policies. Until then, the focus had been almost exclusively on macroeconomics: monetary, aggregate fiscal, and exchange rate policies. The introduction of structural conditions on IMF lending was necessitated by the changing nature of the membership and of the problems that members were facing. Such conditions helped address the underlying causes of weak and unstable economic growth, but they also involved the IMF more deeply in domestic policy debates encompassing political and cultural issues as corollaries of economic issues.

As long as the fund was concerned only with balancing aggregate data and applying the iron laws of economics, one could argue that deficiencies in governance—the peerage gap—would have only minor consequences. When the internal structure of an economy is also on the table—*which* subsidies will be cut, *which* taxes will be raised, *which* sectors ought to be privatized, and so forth—it is much more important to ensure that different points of view about the most desirable kind of world in which to live are adequately represented when that advice is being formulated.

The IMF initiated a major effort to circumscribe its structural conditions by adopting new guidelines in 2002.[12] A recent review of the implementation of those guidelines found evidence of progress in streamlining policy implementation in borrowing countries and of some associated improvements. As more is done to streamline and focus the fund's lending operations, disputes over the concentration of decisionmaking power regarding lending policies should diminish.

COALITION BUILDING. As is often noted in governance debates, the United States is the only country with a veto over major policy decisions of the IMF. A limited number of decisions—such as increases in quotas, sales of gold, allocations of special drawing rights (SDRs), and changes in the size of the executive board—require an 85 percent majority of the total votes, of which the United States currently holds 17 percent. The second-largest share is that of Japan, at just over 6 percent. This disparity obviously confers a status on the United States that is not enjoyed by any of the other 183 member countries.

What is easily forgotten in this catechism is that other members can band together to form coalitions that match or exceed in size the voting power of the United States. The twelve countries that constitute the Euro area hold 23 percent of the voting power in the board of governors,[13] the European Union as a whole holds 32 percent, and the developing countries that constitute the G-24 hold 16 percent.[14] The membership of the IMF therefore consists of a number of minority blocs, any one of which has the potential to use its veto power to influence the outcome of a policy debate. Doing so is complicated when the bloc includes disparate interests, but overcoming those complications requires only the collective will of the group, not a change in global governance.

BOARD LEADERSHIP. A related consideration is that the collective voice of groups of countries with common interests is often weakened by the practice in some constituencies of rotating representation on the executive board among members or of replacing directors every few years. As of mid-2006, half of the twenty-four directors had held office for less than two years, and half of those had replaced directors from a different country. Only four directors had held office for five years or more. Constituencies that have elected the same executive director repeatedly have generally benefited from having an effective and experienced voice at the board. Among developing countries, Alexandre Kafka (Brazil, 1966–98), Abbas Mirakhor (Iran, 1990–present), Ahmed Zaki Saad (Egypt, 1946–70), and Shakour Shaalan (Egypt, 1992–present) are prime examples, and a similar advantage has applied to industrial countries that have retained the same executive director over time, such as Belgium (for example, Jacques de Groote, 1973–94) and the Netherlands (for example, Pieter Lieftinck, 1955–76).

RESTORATION OF BASIC VOTES. In the original design of the IMF, more than 11 percent of total voting power was allocated in the form of an equal number of "basic votes" for each country.[15] The result was a combination of financial and Westphalian principles for determining voting shares. Unfortunately, the Articles of Agreement specified a numeric value (250 per member) for basic votes, to be added to a more flexible number of votes linked to quotas (one vote for each $100,000 of quota).[16] As the quota size of the fund has increased many times over the years, the share of basic votes has dissipated to approximately 2 percent of the total.

The major operational consequence of that downward trend has been to deflate the voting power of the two executive directors from sub-Saharan Africa. Together, they represent forty-three countries, and if basic votes had been retained at 11 percent of the total, they would cast 6.2 percent of the votes. As it is, they cast just 4.4 percent. Numerically, the major counterpart to the decline has been an increase in U.S. voting power by 1.5 percentage points. To reverse the trend by restoring the 11 percent share for basic votes would require an amendment to the Articles of Agreement. At the current level of quotas, the 250 basic votes would have to be raised to 1,450, but a more permanent solution (allowing for future quota increases) would involve replacing the fixed number with a fixed ratio (1:8, as at Bretton Woods) of basic votes to quota-based votes.

DOWNSIZING THE EXECUTIVE BOARD. When the IMF executive board first met in 1946, it had just twelve seats; five directors represented the largest members and the other seven represented groups of countries, which were called constituencies. As the membership grew, it became necessary to increase the number of constituencies to maintain adequate representation for various regions. With the second amendment to the Articles of Agreement in 1978, the size of the board was fixed at twenty seats, with the proviso that the number could be changed temporarily by a vote of at least 85 percent of the board of governors.[17] For each election of executive directors since 1992, the size of the board has been set at twenty-four.

Virtually everyone who has analyzed the effectiveness of the executive board has concluded that twenty-four is too large a number for this type of deliberative and decision-making body.[18] The same conclusion applies to the IMF's ministerial-level advisory body, the International Monetary and Financial Committee (IMFC), which has the same membership as the executive board. Reducing the size of these bodies has nonetheless proved difficult, primarily because states have been reluctant to recombine into new constituencies. Historically, much of the discussion concerned ways to consolidate the chairs of developing countries, a task that proved especially daunting.[19] In the twenty-first century, the focus is squarely on the European Union, as both the most extensively represented region (with six to eight directors) and the one with the clearest path toward consolidation.[20]

Arguably, the EU as a whole does not gain and probably loses influence by holding so many seats on the executive board. The EU's voice is diluted and may be internally conflicted, certainly compared with that of the United States, which speaks with one voice at the board.[21] But that regional consideration clashes with the interests of individual member states, which might have to sacrifice representation for their subregional national interests. Moving beyond this conflict probably requires further progress on the political integration of Europe.

SPECIAL MAJORITIES. The final point to consider on governance concerns the role of special majorities in the IMF. A measure of equalization could be achieved either by reducing the majority required for certain decisions or by reducing the U.S. share of the vote below the level that confers veto power.

As recent debates have illustrated, U.S. veto power—conferred by the requirement for an 85 percent majority for major decisions—has become a lightning rod for criticism of the IMF as a U.S.-dominated organization.[22] Since the United States is by far the largest single source of usable currencies for IMF lending, it is of critical importance to preserve the underpinnings of the country's continued political support. Traditionally, the veto has been a key component, providing assurance to the U.S. Congress that it retains ultimate control over the use of the funds that it authorizes. A question for the future is whether that assurance is worth retaining even if it weakens the effectiveness of the institution.

Does the United States gain from being the only country with a veto over major decisions? In Joseph Nye's terms, it might gain hard power, but it probably loses "soft power" to the extent that the veto increases resentment and resistance to IMF policy advice in borrowing countries that are subject to the fund's loan conditions.[23] To borrow Thomas Friedman's phrase, the world economy has become a lot flatter since 1944, but to many people the IMF still looks like a steep mountain, with the United States sitting at the summit.[24]

Conclusions

The bottom line on governance is that there are many ways to improve upon the status quo. The conflicts between effectiveness and legitimacy and between the requirements for closing the power gap and those for closing the peerage gap are very real, but they are not insurmountable. To overcome those conflicts requires only the broad political will to further the global welfare.

Mustering that political will may have been easier when the IMF was founded than it is today. The IMF was designed at a time when dynamic economic growth was but a distant dream. The driving concerns at Bretton Woods were to avoid a repeat of the conflicts and economic collapse that had devastated the world economy for a quarter-century and to reestablish and maintain multilateral economic and financial relations among nation-states. Those goals have been achieved far more dramatically than the founders could have imagined. Harry Dexter White and John Maynard Keynes would not recognize the world of the twenty-first century, but they surely would be delighted at the overall progress that has been made. But the tiger has dragged in some vermin in its teeth.

The biggest strength but also the biggest flaw in the design of the IMF and of the entire official side of the international financial system is its conservatism. The system is stable, but it also is slow to respond to changes in global conditions and demands. As a result, gaps arise between the areas in which expertise is strongest and those in which the greatest demand for expertise exists or will exist; between the way country groupings form and the way they should form in order to promote economic development; and between the existing structure of global governance and a structure that would engage all countries and regions in a positive relationship with the IMF as an institution. The basic message of this chapter is that because of the inherent conservatism of the system, those gaps are likely to persist, but that through careful adaptation it should be possible to minimize their negative consequences.

Notes

1. World Economic Outlook database (www.imf.org/external/pubs/ft/weo/2000/02/data/index.htm). For an analysis of the causal relation between globalization and improvements in living standards and poverty reduction, see Stanley Fischer, "Globalization and Its Challenges," *American Economic Review* 93, no. 2 (May 2003): 1–30.

2. Of the sixteen countries with the largest voting shares in 2005, all but one (India) were creditors. Of the top fifty members ranked by voting share, thirty-two were creditors; in the bottom fifty, only one (Botswana) was a creditor. In total, the forty-six creditor countries hold more than 78 percent of the voting power in the IMF.

3. See "A Medium-Term Strategy for the IMF: Meeting the Challenge of Globalization" and related papers (www.imf.org/external/np/exr/ib/2006/041806.htm). The strategic review also encompasses operational features of the IMF, including its sources of financing.

4. See James M. Boughton, "The IMF and the Force of History: Ten Events and Ten Ideas That Have Shaped the Institution," IMF Working Paper WP/04/75 (Washington: International Monetary Fund, May 2004).

5. See James M. Boughton, "Does the World Need a Universal Financial Institution?" *World Economics* 6 (April-June 2005): 27–46.

6. Many studies of emerging markets—for example, Christoph Klingen, Beatrice Weder, and Jeromin Zettelmeyer," How Private Creditors Fared in Emerging Debt Markets, 1970–2000," IMF Working Paper WP/04/13 (2004) (www.imf.org/external/pubs/ft/wp/2004/wp0413.pdf)—adopt a narrower definition, usually based on whether a country's external obligations trade in an organized market. Those definitions imply a much smaller number of qualifying countries.

7. Each member country is assigned a quota that affects the size of its financial subscription to the fund, its voting share, its borrowing limits, and its share in allocations of special drawing rights.

8. See Richard Cooper and others, "Report to the IMF Executive Board of the Quota Formula Review Group" (2000) (www.imf.org/external/np/tre/quota/2000/eng/qfrg/report/index.htm); Edwin M. Truman, "Rearranging IMF Chairs and Shares: The Sine Qua Non of IMF Reform," in *Reforming the IMF for the Twenty-First Century*, Special Report 19, edited by Edwin M. Truman (Washington: Institute for International Economics, 2006).

9. See Ariel Buira, ed., *Reforming the Governance of the IMF and the World Bank* (London: Anthem Press, 2005). For an ad hoc procedure aimed at reconciling some aspects of the two gaps, see Vijay Kelkar, Vikash Yadav, and Praveen Chaudhry, "Reforming the Governance of the International Monetary Fund," *World Economy* 27, no. 5 (May 2004): 727–43.

10. International Monetary Fund, *Annual Report 2005* (www.imf.org/external/pubs/ft/ar/2005/eng/index.htm), pp. 53–58.

11. James M. Boughton, *Silent Revolution: The International Monetary Fund 1979–1989* (Washington: International Monetary Fund, 2001), chap. 17.

12. See "Guidelines on Conditionality" (September 25, 2002) and related papers (www.imf.org/External/np/pdr/cond/2002/eng/guid/092302.htm).

13. Voting power in the executive board is more complicated, because constituencies do not coincide with conventional interest groups and because directors are not permitted to split their votes. For a discussion of these complications as they affect the voice and representation of developing countries, see Ngaire Woods and Domenico Lombardi, "Uneven Patterns of Governance: How Developing Countries Are Represented at the IMF," *Review of International Political Economy* 13, no. 3 (August 2006): 480–515. Lorenzo Bini Smaghi, "IMF Governance and the Political Economy of a Consolidated European Seat," in *Reforming the IMF for the Twenty-First Century*, Special Report 19, edited by Edwin M. Truman (Washington: Institute for International Economics, 2006), discusses the complex relationships between voting shares and voting power for various coalitions in the executive board. As noted above, however, voting strength is less relevant in the executive board than in the board of governors.

14. The G-24 total includes China, which has observer status in the group.

15. In relation to the schedule of quotas agreed at Bretton Woods for the forty-four countries represented there, basic votes were fixed at one-eighth of total quota-based

votes, or 11.1 percent of total voting power. Because a few countries declined to join at the outset—including the Soviet Union, with the third-largest assigned quota—basic votes accounted for 11.9 percent of the total for the forty original members.

16. When the Articles of Agreement were amended in 1968, this formula became one vote for each SDR 100,000 of quota.

17. Articles of Agreement, article XII, section 3(b).

18. For example, Peter B. Kenen and others, *International Economic and Financial Cooperation: New Issues, New Actors, New Responses* (Brookings, 2004), and David Peretz, "Assessment of IMF as a Principal Institution for Promoting the Global Public Good of Financial Stability," report prepared for the International Task Force on Global Public Goods (2005) (www.gpgtaskforce.org/bazment.aspx?page_id=175).

19. See, for example, Alexandre Kafka, "Governance of the Fund," in *The International Monetary and Financial System: Developing-Country Perspectives,* edited by Gerald K. Helleiner (New York: St. Martin's Press, 1996).

20. France, Germany, and the United Kingdom appoint directors, and Belgium, Italy, and the Netherlands have always elected their own nationals as directors for mixed constituencies. The Nordic constituency is sometimes represented by a director from an EU member (Denmark, Finland, or Sweden), and Spain rotates an elected chair with Mexico and Venezuela.

21. See Bini Smaghi, "IMF Governance and the Political Economy of a Consolidated European Seat."

22. See Nancy Birdsall, "Why It Matters Who Runs the IMF and the World Bank," in *Globalization and the Nation State: The Impact of the IMF and the World Bank,* edited by Gustav Ranis, James Raymond Vreeland, and Stephen Kosack (London and New York: Routledge, 2006); Ariel Buira, "The Governance of the IMF in a Global Economy," in Ariel Buira, ed., *Challenges to the IMF and the World Bank: Developing Country Perspectives* (London: Anthem Press, 2003), pp. 13–36; Leo Van Houtven, *Governance of the IMF: Decision Making, Institutional Oversight, Transparency, and Accountability,* Pamphlet 53 (Washington: International Monetary Fund, 2002).

23. Joseph S. Nye Jr., "Soft Power," *Foreign Policy* 80 (Autumn 1990): 153–71.

24. Thomas L. Friedman, *The World Is Flat: A Brief History of the Twenty-First Century* (New York: Farrar, Strauss, and Giroux, 2005).

3

The World Bank:
Toward a Global Club

NANCY BIRDSALL

The World Bank can be thought of as a particular type of global club, with a structure close to that of a credit union in which the members are nations.[1] Its mission, as originally conceived—to promote broadly shared and sustainable global prosperity—serves the common interests of all its country members. The World Bank is not, of course, the only global club (the largest in number of members is obviously the United Nations), and it is not the only credit union whose members are countries—there are, for example, regional development banks, the European Investment Bank, and, for some aspects of development, the International Monetary Fund. However, it is the only truly global club that has the financial structure of a credit union. Let us think of it for the purposes of this chapter as a "global credit club."

This chapter is based heavily on excerpts from Nancy Birdsall, "A Global Credit Club, Not Another Development Agency," in *Rescuing the World Bank: A CGD Working Group Report and Selected Essays,* edited by Nancy Birdsall (Washington: Center for Global Development, 2006), 69–85.

Bretton Woods: Creating a Credit Club, Not a Development Agency

The financing mechanism conceived by John Maynard Keynes, Harry Dexter White, and others at Bretton Woods in 1944 for this global credit club did not rely on "contributions" to finance "transfers" from rich to poor nations (although, of course, the club members created a separate club for that purpose later, called the International Development Association (IDA), in which only the rich country contributors have membership rights).[2] Keynes and his colleagues did not invent a development agency, and they did not conceive of the resulting financing as a transfer. On the contrary, the borrowers (at that time primarily Western Europeans) were thought of as full members and partners in the venture.

In the light of this simple idea of the bank as a global credit club, what are the issues that arise with respect to its current governance structure? How might various proposals for reform strengthen the bank by returning it to its spirit as a "club of nations" whose objectives are shared by all club members?

In the World Bank "club," different members have different amounts of "deposits" and provide different amounts of guarantees. The biggest depositor is the U.S. government, and the United States, Japan, and Germany are the World Bank's biggest guarantors. The rich country guarantors back all the borrowing from this credit union of member countries, whether the credit union makes good loans or bad loans and whether member country borrowers pay up or not (though history indicates that only rarely do they fail to pay on time).[3] The guarantees (and perhaps the extraordinarily low default rate) mean that this credit union, even with relatively low deposits in the form of paid-in capital, can borrow outside at good rates and lend at good rates to its less wealthy members.

The founders in short conceived of a global club that, at low financial cost to the big depositors and guarantors (only the United States at that time, for all practical purposes), would reduce borrowing costs for the poorer members (at that time war-torn European countries) and make the world a richer and safer place.

The boundaries within which the club would operate were well understood and fully embraced by the members at the World Bank's founding. The club was established to promote an open and liberal international economic system, based on market-driven growth and trade—in notable contrast to the system espoused by the Soviet Union, in 1944 a wartime ally. It would do so by helping the war-ravaged countries of Europe—and the poorer countries of

Asia, Latin America, and Africa—to finance investments that would enable them to prosper as partners in this open system, in the interests of global stability and security.

Today: An Aid Agency?

It is surprising how far the World Bank of today has strayed, in spirit at least, from its original conception. Today the bank has "borrowers" (the developing countries) and "non-borrowers" (the advanced countries). The bank's mission is now framed explicitly as reducing global poverty—by which is meant poverty in borrowing countries—not as supporting and encouraging global prosperity and security through trade and investment in an open, liberal global economy.[4] Of course, market-led growth and poverty reduction generally are mutually reinforcing. So what is the practical difference between a credit club whose objective is to promote shared global prosperity in an open, liberal economy and a development agency whose objective is to battle poverty? Perhaps the key difference that has emerged over more than fifty years is that between a cooperative whose common mission is in every member's interest (global security and prosperity in an open system) and an aid agency in which some parties "contribute," in principle to "help" others.

The fact is that the distinction between club and aid agency, subtle as it may be, is important to the future of the World Bank. The bank is under tremendous pressure today. It is assailed by those on the left for lack of *legitimacy*—for promoting privileged "insider" financial and corporate interests instead of addressing the needs of the voiceless poor. It is assailed by those on the right for its refusal to admit to its lost *relevance*. With increasing flows of private capital to the developing world (and ample reserves in China, India, and many other emerging markets), they question the use of public resources to subsidize loans in those settings. Private markets and private transfers would be more efficient and effective.[5] Those at the center, inside as well as outside the World Bank, criticize the bank for its lack of *effectiveness* in attacking poverty in the poorest countries, for its lack of agility in responding to the real demands of its large- and middle-income borrowers (and thus its apparent loss of relevance), and for its loss of institutional focus as it responds to ever-expanding demands from (ironically, some would say) its more powerful members: demands to do everything from assessing needs in Gaza and Iraq, to managing a global program to "fast-track" education gains, to piloting cross-border trade in carbon emissions rights.

The pressures have to do with three problems: erosion of the bank's legitimacy as an institution, loss of faith in its effectiveness (in reducing poverty and promoting "balanced and externally oriented growth"), and its apparent growing irrelevance. Might the bank's shareholders, especially the United States, be better positioned to address these problems by embracing a vision of the bank as a club rather than a development agency? How might a return to the spirit of Bretton Woods, to the idea of a global credit club, change the outline of the current debates among the bank's critics about the institution? What would be the implications of a return to the spirit of Bretton Woods for reform of the bank's governance?

Legitimacy: Member Voice and Vote

How did the founders make the idea of a global credit club operational? They agreed that in their club, voting power would be related to members' "dues" (or deposits and guarantees) and that the dues would be broadly related to members' financial capacity. However, they wanted to avoid creating a perfect one-to-one relationship between financial capacity and influence in the club. On the one hand, members taking greater risk ought to have a substantial say in the rules and practices of the club, if only to secure their continued financial commitment. On the other hand, the overwhelming financial capacity of a very few countries to take that risk, if reflected fully in the allocation of votes, would undermine the spirit of a club. As Harry Dexter White of the United States noted at the time, referring to the International Monetary Fund (IMF), "to accord voting power strictly proportionate to the value of the subscription would give the one or two powers control over the Fund. To do that would destroy the truly international character of the Fund, and seriously jeopardize its success."[6]

Therefore, in the case of the World Bank and the IMF, the founders introduced such mechanisms as "basic votes," which were distributed equally to all members (in the bank, each member has 250 votes irrespective of shares, plus one additional vote for each share), and double majority voting (of shares and of member countries) to make certain fundamental changes in the Articles of Agreement.

The idea was that the country taking the main risk—at that time the United States—would define the key boundaries within which the club would operate. At the same time, to preserve the spirit of a club and to ensure that the club would be effective, other members, including active borrowers (initially the Europeans), would have opportunities to influence, within those boundaries, specific priorities, policies, and detailed practices. On some key issues, they also would have the ability to resist changes that might reflect only the narrow interests of a few powerful members.

Over time, however, the ability of the bank's (initially mostly European) borrowers to affect the bank's priorities, policies, and practices has eroded. Today there are many more borrowers. In 1947–48 the bank made loans to six countries (France, the Netherlands, Denmark, Luxembourg, Chile, and India); the International Bank for Reconstruction and Development (IBRD) and the IDA now lend to almost 150 countries. And the world has changed in another respect. The political mechanisms of representation and voice in "democracies" and in international "clubs" of nations are now almost universally acknowledged as ideal in their own right (*Development as Freedom*, to use the title of Amartya Sen's book) and as effective in an instrumental sense—for promoting sustainable growth and reducing poverty because they demand accountability and provide checks on abuses of power. The idea of political freedom in a democracy is also now closely associated with the economic model of open markets and thus with the original "mission" of the club. These changes in norms have put pressure on the bank to function more in the manner envisioned at its founding.

The result is growing demand for reform of governance at the bank, especially to ensure much greater representation—in terms of voting power, board membership, staffing, and so on—of developing country borrowers, who are the members most affected by bank policies and practices. The spirit of an international club is particularly resonant in proposals for

—the current president of the bank to "push the Bank's member governments to make the Bank's governance more representative and thus more legitimate" and, as a first concrete step, to ask the bank governors to call for an independent assessment, to be made public, of voting shares and board representation, including options for changes[7]

—the current president of the bank to commit now to a more open and transparent process for selection of his successor, including by asking the bank governors to formalize a credible, rule-based process[8]

—use of double majority voting on many more issues to create an incentive for borrowers—who now see no point in debating institutional issues over which they have no influence—to build coalitions[9]

—a governance structure for a trust fund for global public goods at the bank in which middle- and low-income borrowers would have at least 50 percent of the votes, with the middle-income countries having more power to set the agenda in return for the financing that they would provide by paying higher interest charges on their loans than they otherwise would[10]

—a rethinking of the "framework" for the IDA (the bank's facility for low-cost loans and grants to the poorest countries, funded by direct contributions from donors), separate from any reconfiguration of IBRD shares (which would have little impact on decisionmaking in the IDA), so that both borrowers and non-borrowers would "feel more ownership."[11]

With a more representative governance structure and broader engagement of borrowers, the bank would be returning to the original conception of its founders—in which borrowers and non-borrowers were full members of the club—and it would command more legitimacy as a global institution. It would still be a credit club, in which the big depositors have more say. But it also would provide much greater incentives for borrowing members to engage on key issues. To quote White once again: "Indeed it is very doubtful if many countries would be willing to participate in an international organization with wide powers if one or two countries were able to control its policies."[12]

Effectiveness in the Low-Income IDA Member Countries

In 1960 the bank's rich country non-borrowers established the IDA window at the bank for lending to the poorest countries at highly concessional interest rates. IDA lending is financed by outright contributions of the rich countries, creating what could be considered an "aid agency" inside the existing club.

The bank's effectiveness in the world's poorest countries is today highly questionable and increasingly questioned.[13] In the case of the IDA window, failure of the bank's shareholders to address the governance problem is undermining the bank's institutional effectiveness. Without governance reform, or at least reform of the IDA itself, the bank risks additional erosion not only of its legitimacy but its effectiveness, particularly in the poorest, most aid-dependent countries.[14]

Having learned the hard way that policies that are imposed or even simply "suggested" from outside often do not stick, the bank, along with virtually all official creditors and donors, is now committed to the principle of developing country "ownership" of their own policies and reforms. Yet as long as the bank itself is not seen as co-owned and legitimate in developing countries, it is too easy for bank-financed programs to become controversial and difficult for developing country leaders—enlightened and reform-minded as they may be—to implement. The plight of bank adjustment programs (and of the benighted "Washington Consensus" reforms in general) is a compelling example.[15] Bank programs become politically controversial not only because they create losers as well as winners (which cannot be avoided), but because they are seen as being imposed from outside.

Returning to the spirit of Bretton Woods might help. In a club—but not in an aid agency—the recipients of financing have the power that comes with membership, and their agreement is more obviously required on the broad policies and practices that govern the club's operations.

Relevance: China, India, and Middle-Income Countries

Many observers argue that the World Bank should stop lending altogether to China, India, and many middle-income countries, on the grounds of the irrelevance of such lending in a world of sophisticated private markets. That argument is strengthened by the fact that China, among others, is awash in reserves—and is still transferring capital to the United States, rather than receiving capital from the United States and other capital-rich advanced economies.[16] There are counterarguments, including the volatility of markets, which puts middle-income borrowers who rely on private markets at risk in the event of a global crisis; the poor access to private markets of some poor and middle-income countries (such as Paraguay, Ecuador, and Morocco); and the broad-based analytical capacity that the bank brings to issues of global importance, such as protection of biodiversity. The report of the Center for Global Development Working Group notes also the legitimate interest of the rich country non-borrowers in promoting equitable growth in the countries where two-thirds of the world's poor live as well as their legitimate interest in supporting their own prosperity and security.[17]

Various proposals have been made to help the bank retain its relevance and build greater allegiance among its middle-income members. Those proposals emphasize the need for risk sharing and other products to catalyze private flows to countries and reduction of the political or financial costs of the "hassle" associated with borrowing from the bank, whether due to excessive fiduciary obligations, including those to limit corruption; to excessive safeguards against environmental and other costs; or to excessive delays between requesting and receiving a loan. Similarly, Jessica Einhorn suggests that the bank's members agree to lock in now a twenty-five-year sunset clause for loan disbursements as an incentive for the bank management and bureaucracy to adapt to the creative challenge of developing new non-loan services for middle-income countries more quickly.[18]

If we conceive of the bank as a club, managed by its members for their own benefit, then the substantive merits of these arguments and proposals for change, one way or another, yield to the question of whether particular members wish to avail themselves of the benefits of membership under existing conditions or use their influence to change those conditions—or perhaps do both. If China wants to borrow at the cost already agreed to by all members, for whatever reason (including because China trusts the bank's technical input more if it is bundled with a financial commitment), then so be it. If a country (Korea in 1998) that had eschewed borrowing for many years asks the bank for a loan during an emergency, then so be it. If non-borrowers wish to limit the subsidy implied in loans to relatively richer or more liquid (in terms of reserves) middle-income members, then they have the option of proposing a policy of smaller subsidies (higher interest charges on loans) for the relatively richer borrowers.[19]

To put it another way, let the members of the club decide. That, in effect, is the current situation—though it may reflect the inertia of failed cooperation as much as a positive decision. An interesting issue arises because some members, particularly the borrowers, have limited influence in changing the conditions (pricing, delays, conditions, and safeguards) under which they now participate as members. In that sense, the question of whether the bank can return to its roots as a global club may well bear on the question of whether it continues to be relevant in its current form for a large group of its members. In the absence of voice, some members may in effect choose the option of exit.[20]

Concluding Note

The problems of legitimacy, effectiveness, and relevance at the World Bank are all rooted in the failure of its members to adjust its governance structure to the economic, social, and normative changes in the global system over the last fifty years—and to "globalization" itself. One advantage of the L-20 concept discussed elsewhere in this book is that less institutional and more informal periodic interchange among heads of both rich and developing countries—the idea of the L-20—may be the best single substitute in the short run for politically difficult formal changes at the bank. It might also provide the best setting for promoting a franker and more productive discourse that might finally inspire the fundamental changes in governance that so far have eluded the bank's members.

Notes

1. The word "club" has different connotations in different cultures and settings. I use it in the everyday North American sense, which implies open membership, not exclusivity—for example, the local Rotary Club, not the country club.

2. The global credit club was the brilliant invention of U.K. economist Keynes, along with the American Harry Dexter White and their colleagues from forty-two other countries who conceived the World Bank and the International Monetary Fund at the Bretton Woods Conference in 1944.

3. The relevance of the non-borrowers' guarantees to the bank's ability to borrow and borrowing costs is sometimes questioned, because bank financial policies since the early 1970s have included substantial provisioning and reserves and because it has been so rare that borrowers have delayed repayment, let alone defaulted. Since more than 80 percent of the bank's current reserves come from transfers from net income and only a small minority from paid-in capital, there is a sense in which the borrowers can now be said to be contributing to the bank's low borrowing cost and financial solidity. From the beginning, of course, the guarantees, like the nuclear option, were useful only when not used.

4. To quote Jessica Einhorn in "Reforming the World Bank," *Foreign Affairs* 84, no. 1 (January-February 2006): 17–21: "Over time, the Bank has evolved from an organization focused on growth through trade and investment to an organization set on achieving a world without poverty. *Its core mission is no longer to partner with . . . countries in their pursuit of balanced and externally oriented growth; it is to alleviate poverty*" [emphasis added]. And to quote from a working group report sponsored by the Center for Global Development: "The Bank's mission is to reduce poverty in developing countries." CGD Working Group, "The Hardest Job in the World: Five Crucial Tasks for the New President of the World Bank," in *Rescuing the World Bank: A CGD Working Group Report and Selected Essays*, edited by Nancy Birdsall (Washington: Center for Global Development, 2006), pp. 1–65, quote on p. 15. The newer conception is not entirely recent. The non-borrowers established the IDA window in 1960. The speech of Robert McNamara, the bank's fifth president, in Nairobi in 1973 perhaps marks the official birth of the "poverty" mission for the IBRD and the bank group as a whole. Up to that time the World Bank was primarily a financier of bricks-and-mortar projects, with investment in infrastructure seen as the key to open, market-based growth. By the time of James Wolfensohn, the poverty objective had matured and was captured aptly in an inscription in the lobby of the bank's main building—"Our dream is a world free of poverty"—and in a noteworthy increase in the proportion of bank lending for social programs.

5. See CGD Working Group, "The Hardest Job in the World," for more detail and for citations to these critiques.

6. Joseph Gold, *Voting and Decisions in the International Monetary Fund: An Essay on the Law and Practice of the Fund* (Washington: International Monetary Fund, 1972), p. 19.

7. CGD Working Group, "The Hardest Job in the World," pp. 44–50.

8. Ibid., p. 48.

9. Ngaire Woods, "The Battle for the Bank," in *Rescuing the World Bank,* edited by Birdsall, p. 101.

10. CGD Working Group, "The Hardest Job in the World," pp. 42–44.

11. Masood Ahmed, "Votes and Voice: Reforming Governance at the World Bank," in *Rescuing the World Bank,* edited by Birdsall, p. 93.

12. Gold, *Voting and Decisions in the International Monetary Fund,* p. 19.

13. See William Easterly, "The World Bank and Low-Income Countries: The Escalating Agenda," pp. 103–108, and Steven Radelet, "The Role of the Bank in Low-Income Countries," pp. 109–15, in *Rescuing the World Bank,* edited by Birdsall, for a summary of the central issues.

14. On this point, see Kemal Dervis, with Ceren Ozer, *A Better Globalization: Legitimacy, Governance, and Reform* (Washington: Center for Global Development, 2005) and Ahmed, "Votes and Voice: Reforming Governance at the World Bank."

15. William Easterly, "What Did Structural Adjustment Adjust? The Association of Policies and Growth with Repeated IMF and World Bank Adjustment Loans," CGD Working Paper 11 (Washington: Center for Global Development, 2002), among other studies, documents the failures.

16. The irrelevance argument is set out in Adam Lerrick, "Has the World Bank Lost Control?" in *Rescuing the World Bank,* edited by Birdsall, pp. 117–32.

17. See CGD Working Group, "The Hardest Job in the World," and David de Ferranti, "The World Bank and the Middle-Income Countries," in *Rescuing the World Bank,* edited by Birdsall, pp. 133–51.

18. Einhorn, "Reforming the World Bank."

19. A key rationale for the Gurria-Volcker Commission's recommendation of differential loan pricing was to encourage graduation of richer borrowers with access to private markets. See Commission on the Role of the MDBs in Emerging Markets, *The Role of the Multilateral Development Banks in Emerging Market Economies: Findings of the Commission on the Role of the MDBs in Emerging Markets* (Washington: Carnegie Endowment for International Peace, 2001). For a different view, see the recommendations in the report approved by a majority of the Meltzer Commission, "Report of the International Financial Institution Advisory Commission," chaired by Allan H. Meltzer (2000).

20. The risk that China and other Asian nations will set up a regional monetary fund is currently the key impetus for the United States and Europe to agree to some change in IMF quotas. A similar situation might arise at the bank, though in less dramatic form and creating less immediate pressure on non-borrowers.

4

United Nations Reform

ANN FLORINI AND CARLOS PASCUAL

The fifty-one countries that founded the United Nations in 1945 meant to create an organization that would save the world from the kind of global catastrophe that they had endured twice in three decades—a major war among nations. The leaders of those countries based their design for the organization on the prevailing realities of their time. Nation-states were by far the most important, if not the only, significant actors on the international scene and certainly the only ones that could cause large-scale violence and make decisions to avoid it. Their relationships with one another depended at root on their relative national power, defined primarily in terms of military strength. Threats to any country would come primarily from other countries, and an adequate response required something other than a competing national alliance—it demanded a world alliance against such threats to global interests. More than six decades later, those assumptions no longer hold, and the threats confronting the international community challenge it to update the UN system and to revise how the UN relates to regional and bilateral organizations.

This chapter reviews the dramatic changes in the nature of the problems confronting the international community and the resulting gaps in its capacity to tackle those problems. It assesses the efforts to adapt and reform the UN leading up to the 2005 world summit and the lessons learned in the process, and it concludes with key questions that need to be addressed to guide the next stage of UN reform. The chapter does not attempt to provide definitive answers on what a "reformed" UN should look like, a task that would require a much more extensive treatment. Instead, we offer suggestions on how to move toward a more viable reform process, based on two observations. The first observation is that the UN's vast membership has diverse goals for UN reform. To date, most member countries have pursued those issues of greatest self-interest, taking extreme positions on them in order to increase their negotiating leverage. If that trend continues, UN reform will be forever frozen. Nations will need to make trade-offs across their areas of interest and agree on a compromise package that, while it gives no individual member everything it wants, makes all members better off. Negotiating an acceptable package has proven to be beyond the capacity of an institutional process that involves 191 countries. A process by which the L-20 countries would agree upon and then support a comprehensive package might stand a better chance of reducing the complexities of negotiations to a more manageable level. If the UN's member countries do not accept such an approach, then they need to consider whether they are willing to accept the cost of a multilateral system that is not suited to addressing the problems of its time and that will leave all nations disappointed and disillusioned.

The second observation is that transnational threats such as international terrorism or the proliferation of weapons of mass destruction underscore the need for effective multilateral institutions because, as argued below, no single nation can insulate itself from or effectively address those threats alone. If multilateral institutions do not adapt to address today's threats more effectively, those institutions will not be used and they will become increasingly irrelevant. That, of course, would be the worst possible outcome, as it would suit the interests of no country. But it is the default position toward which the international community seems to be heading.

The Changing Nature of International Threats and Challenges

The nature of international relations and security issues has changed fundamentally since the end of World War II, especially since the end of the cold war, but the structure and rules of the UN have not. It is no wonder that policymakers end up frustrated with the UN. At times that frustration has led to attempts to bypass the UN or to disregard it when its processes are too cumbersome or its decisions inconvenient. That has resulted in serious costs for the UN and for those who have chosen to act outside multilateral structures, particularly the United States. The UN has been made weaker. And the United States has paid a price, too—for example, in the perceived illegitimacy of its intervention in Iraq. That has made it all the harder to mobilize the international engagement needed to sustain a transition process in Iraq over the decade, at least, that it will need to last. To understand the nature of the problem with the UN and eventually to reform it, one needs to appreciate the changed global environment in which we live. When the UN was created, a fundamental premise was that nation-states were rational actors and that bringing them together in an environment of mutual scrutiny would help avoid the most egregious forms of aggression among states. This basic premise was sound, and war between countries has indeed become far rarer. But interstate war is no longer the primary problem. Rogue states, non-state actors, and sub-state entities often cannot be counted on to act in accordance with the norms traditionally espoused by nation-states, especially if their interest is in seeking attention or power rather than advancing the overall interests of a population. Nation-states cannot be assumed to control developments within their territory. Even the nature of national borders has changed, as technology, finance, communications, and markets have become global in their reach. Conflict also has changed. Today the term "cold war" is most analogous to international attempts to curb Iran's and North Korea's nuclear weapons ambitions. The challenges among "powers" have more to do with managing the rise of emerging powers like China and India than with ideological clashes between superpowers. And violence is more likely to involve internal conflict within states or between state and non-state actors than the kind of interstate conflict that characterized World War II.

These fundamental changes have not gone unnoticed. UN secretary-general Kofi Annan commissioned a high-level panel of international policy experts precisely to develop a better understanding of the nature of the new threats with which the UN is expected to deal. That panel argued that the new global environment presented six major threats to international peace and prosperity:

—poverty, disease, and environmental degradation
—civil war and genocide and other human-inflicted atrocities
—interstate conflict
—proliferation of nuclear, radiological, chemical, and biological weapons
—terrorism
—transnational organized crime.[1]

Like any such list, the panel's list leaves room for argument. Insecurity over energy supplies, for example, could be identified as a separate challenge that could destabilize nations, thrusting them into destructive clashes that might strengthen dictators, undermine international law, threaten fledgling democracies, and redefine the incentives driving international politics. But the report clearly shows the varied sources of significant degradation of human life that have occurred in the last decade and are likely to continue in the next: HIV/AIDS; wars in Iraq, Afghanistan, Sudan, and Congo; terrorist acts throughout the world; and the ability of rogue states to wield unprecedented power as they flaunt international nonproliferation regimes.

Most important, the panel argued that combating these threats requires nations to work together for their collective security through a more effective United Nations. The rationale for collective security, it argued, is threefold. First, these threats recognize no national boundaries; they are interconnected, regardless of distance. The terrorist acts of 9/11, for example, threw 10 million more people into poverty by shutting down international travel and markets. Severe acute respiratory syndrome (SARS) infected 8,000 people in thirty countries in three months. Second, no state can make itself invulnerable, no matter how strong and powerful it might be, as terrorist attacks in New York, Washington, London, Bali, New Delhi, and Madrid have so painfully demonstrated. Third, states will not always meet their responsibility to protect their people; when states fail in that responsibility, the international community has the right to intervene to fulfill that fundamental protective role.[2] Darfur best illustrates such a tragedy, with about 2 million people displaced internally, about 200,000 forced to flee into Chad, and the estimated number of deaths nearing half a million.[3]

The key conclusion is inescapable: all countries have a self-interest in creating a more effective system of international governance that addresses the global and interdependent nature of the international security environment. By investing in such a system of governance, nations might stand a better chance of combating threats that they cannot conquer on their own. Yet all efforts to date to reform the UN and the rules of international governance have fallen short of meeting that objective. Even a cursory look at a few examples helps to illustrate that the cost of failure is severe and that the international community is ill-prepared to cope with existing and emerging risks.

Examples of Failure

Individual nations might convincingly argue why they cannot support specific changes in the rules or architecture of the UN system. But the result has been a stalemate that has made all nations worse off. The impact is not just theoretical. In some cases millions of lives are at risk. In other cases the UN system has become paralyzed, unable to defuse problems before they become crises. Three examples—Darfur, Pakistan, and nuclear proliferation—illustrate the dilemmas that have emerged.

DARFUR. Virtually all UN member states agree that the tragic loss of life in Darfur must be stopped, yet the response of the international community has been ineffectual. The United States characterized the violence in Darfur as genocide in 2004. Thirteen UN Security Council resolutions have condemned the ongoing conflict, including four resolutions that have called for sanctions. The international community, particularly the United States, has provided massive amounts of humanitarian aid, yet the assistance given has met only about 50 percent of estimated needs. The African Union (AU) has dispatched almost 7,000 troops to Darfur, and the situation would be tragically worse if it had not. Yet they are underequipped, many are ill trained, and they have not been able to stop the fighting. When the AU sought NATO and EU assistance to transport troops to the region, the two organizations bickered for weeks over which would take the lead when neither had the capacity to provide the needed capacity on its own.

As of mid-2006, the UN had voted to take over the mission in Darfur from the AU, but it has not succeeded in getting the government of Sudan to accept the change. Even if the UN could begin to deploy immediately, it could take a year or more to deploy a force of 20,000—given that it could not find and mobilize sufficient troops to deploy a force of 13,000 to southern Sudan eighteen months after the signing of a peace agreement. Complicating matters further, there is no peace to keep in Darfur. International efforts to broker an agreement under the "Abuja process" resulted in a document signed by the government of Sudan and the main rebel group, but other rebels rejected the agreement. In the meantime, virtually no resources have been made available to address the root causes of the conflict, such as land, water, and grazing rights. The lesson: even when the international community largely agrees on the problem, there is little agreement on what to do or how to do it, and there is no capacity to carry out the "right to protect" and to deploy peacekeepers in adequate numbers. That leaves the international community unable to address the root causes of conflict and build an effective peace.

PAKISTAN. Most nations readily agree that it is better to prevent a crisis than to have to respond to one. The case of Pakistan, where the warning signs of the confluence of internal and transnational threats are flashing brightly, illustrates that there is little capacity in the UN system to assess and address threats of conflict and instability with wide regional and global implications. It can be argued that Pakistan has the most serious concentration of the six potential threats identified by the high-level UN panel: cross-border terrorism from Afghanistan, pockets of religious extremism, organized crime associated with the Afghan drug trade, conflict with India over Kashmir, internal political tensions and income inequalities exacerbated by the 2005 earthquake, nuclear weapons, and a history of proliferation of nuclear weapons technology. The presence of 18,500 U.S. and NATO forces in Afghanistan brings these risks into even sharper focus, as a crisis in Pakistan could quickly drag in foreign troops.[4]

Despite the level of risk, multilateral agencies have not engaged to help Pakistan defuse a potential crisis. The international community provided extensive humanitarian aid after the devastating earthquake, but it has focused on relief and reconstruction and has not fundamentally redressed the root causes of poverty and inequality. The United States cooperates with Pakistan on counterterrorism activities, but U.S. officials also express frustration over the level of Pakistani political will.[5] Pakistan, meanwhile, seems to try to lower the profile of its counterterrorism operations because only about 25 percent of the population views the U.S. favorably.[6] There are no effective channels for multilateral cooperation on counterterrorism. Pakistan's nuclear program remains beyond formal international controls. The international community has also been relegated to a reactive role in the Kashmir conflict. The lesson: even when the warning signs point to a looming crisis that can destabilize a major country with nuclear weapons and the surrounding region, there are few multilateral tools to mitigate the danger. Especially when sources of instability are internal or there is a strong (even if vulnerable) state, the international community has few means to become systematically engaged, even if unrest or instability would have immediate international consequences.

NUCLEAR PROLIFERATION. India, Iran, and North Korea present three radically different cases, yet all three have circumvented the Nuclear Nonproliferation Treaty, and the international community is grappling in each case with how to deal with the consequences. Because India is a democracy, it presents the least controversial case. Yet under its agreement with the United States, eight of its twenty-two reactors would not come under International Atomic Energy Agency (IAEA) safeguards, and India would be able to import fuel for civilian reactors, thereby freeing up domestically enriched uranium for its weapons program. Iran, as of early October 2006, continued to reject an international offer for a civilian nuclear reactor and fuel supplies, claiming that it cannot relinquish "its right" to enrich uranium. North Korea has already produced nuclear weapons and tested a device; the longer the stalemate in international negotiations lasts, the more time it has to increase its arsenal.

Each of these cases will be resolved differently, but their net impact could be to make irrelevant the principal international measures conceived to curb further proliferation. Non-nuclear states have argued that the nuclear powers must accelerate the reduction of their nuclear weapons, but international dynamics make it politically difficult for nuclear countries to reduce their arsenals when other nations are acquiring nuclear status. Few nations presently have an interest in more intensive inspections under the model additional protocol for IAEA safeguards. It is impossible to offer nations guaranteed supplies of nuclear fuel at market rates if they will not subject themselves to international protocols. The United States and Russia have proposed some ideas on how to move forward, including limiting the number of IAEA-authorized suppliers of fissile material and offering to reprocess spent fuel in Russia. That said, there is no international consensus on the use of inspections, market forces, regulations, or sanctions to prevent fissile material production.

To be sure, the cases of Darfur, Pakistan, and nuclear proliferation are far more complicated than can be addressed here. But they illustrate a point: even when the threats to human life or the international community are poignantly real, the UN (and the multilateral system) has not developed the capacity to deal with them effectively. Moreover, competing interests among UN member states further complicate their ability to reach consensus on needed changes in the UN system. Some nations focus completely on the issue of representation and Security Council reform and refuse to compromise on other matters. Poor and rich countries both care about poverty, but some focus on resource targets to support the Millennium Development Goals and others on governance capacity and the political will to reform. Nations have not agreed on a definition of "terrorism," although doing so might serve to unify counterterrorism efforts, and they lack consensus on whether preemptive force can be used legitimately. Nations also split on the issue of organized crime, some focusing on the need for eradication and others on the need for alternative livelihoods. As a result, no consensus has been reached, and the status quo is perpetuated.

If there is one lesson to be drawn, it may be that all nations need to compromise. There is no "right" answer on how to make trade-offs on building the UN's capacity to address these threats. If each nation stakes out its own interests or insists on a maximal position, constructive changes will never be achieved. Hence, in order to move forward, it is worth looking back to try to understand where compromise failed before and to suggest ideas that could lead to a viable package across issues that would create the prospect of enhancing collective security.

Understanding the UN's Roles and Capabilities

As the world has transformed itself over the past six decades, the UN has served as its dumping ground for an enormous agenda of problems. For example, the UN is now struggling to manage more than 70,000 troops and civilians drawn from more than 100 countries and deployed in eighteen missions in some of the world's most desperate conflict zones—Congo, Liberia, Haiti, and Sudan. The UN deals with more than 19 million people displaced from their homes by violence or natural disaster. Of late, it has been overseeing global efforts to assist millions of tsunami victims, and it toils to call the world's attention to some twenty "forgotten emergencies" that threaten millions more.

But all that activity rests on a fundamentally unsound institutional base. At its core, the UN consists of four parts: the Security Council, the General Assembly, the Economic and Social Council, and the Secretariat, headed by the secretary-general. The fifteen-country Security Council, the only UN body with teeth, gives lopsided power to the victors in World War II, allowing China, France, Russia, the United Kingdom, and the United States each to single-handedly veto any decision. The General Assembly, wherein all 191 UN member countries theoretically have equal voice and power, has degenerated into a Byzantine chamber of largely pointless debates on an endless array of issues large and small. The fifty-three-member Economic and Social Council is, if anything, less effective than the General Assembly. The Secretariat—the staff arm of the UN—is hobbled by extreme micromanagement by member states and a long-standing tradition of weak general management and oversight within the Secretariat.

These core bodies, all established under the UN Charter, in turn are connected in various ways to a wider range of semi-independent programs and funds, such as the United Nations Development Program, the United Nations Environment Program, and the World Food Program. Each has an independent governing body, but the personnel fall to some degree under the authority of the secretary-general. They generally receive little if any funding from the UN's core budget (which consists of dues assessed on member countries in rough correlation to their share of the world economy), relying primarily on voluntary contributions by member states.

A third ring of international bodies consists of the fully independent specialized agencies—the International Atomic Energy Agency, the International Monetary Fund, the World Bank, and so on through the alphabet soup of international organizations. Although nominally part of the UN "system," in practice these are fully autonomous organizations whose work is at best loosely and sporadically coordinated with the UN proper or with other international organizations.

In short, the UN system—established by the world's governments to address global issues—is messy, badly managed, and poorly coordinated. Its flaws have not gone unnoticed. In fact, calls for reform began almost from the UN's birth: the first U.S. Senate investigation of poor UN performance dates back to the 1940s. Since then, waves of UN reform efforts have regularly crashed upon the largely unyielding shores of Turtle Bay, the site of UN headquarters in New York.

As indicated earlier, Secretary-General Kofi Annan launched the most recent reform effort by charging a high-level panel of well-known and well-connected international figures with developing a "grand bargain" for UN reform that would transform the organization into something capable of addressing the far different world of the twenty-first century. In short, Annan was pushing for a reform package that would include

—Security Council expansion

—greater financial support by rich member countries for the development programs of the poorer members

—significant management reform of the Secretariat

—a clear legal definition of terrorism

—progress on nonproliferation of weapons of mass destruction

—replacement of the discredited Human Rights Commission by a significantly different Human Rights Council

—creation of a Peacebuilding Commission intended to create some unity of effort across the UN system and with key donors, troop contributors, and affected parties

—some new thinking on how to make the entire UN system more coherent.

All this was to be agreed on in September 2005, when the vast majority of the world's heads of government were to gather for a world summit in conjunction with the annual opening session of the General Assembly. Supporters of the "grand bargain" approach felt that only through such an overarching framework could meaningful progress occur. Different UN members care about very different parts of this package of reforms, and they rarely show much interest in one another's concerns.

The United States government, which contributes 22 percent of the UN's core budget and 27 percent of the peacekeeping budget, has long shown itself willing to throw its considerable weight around in pursuit of its goals for UN reform. It had three primary interests. The executive branch cared intensely about terrorism and nonproliferation, wanting in particular an agreed definition of terrorism that would have ramifications for international agreements and the ability of international organizations to take action on terrorism. The U.S. Congress, some of whose members have long condemned the UN as a cesspool of corruption and incompetence, insisted on significant steps on management reform. Both branches felt strongly that the Human Rights Commission had become a significant embarrassment, serving more as a protector of human rights abusers than as a source of progress on human rights, and wanted it scrapped.

Developing countries have long seen the UN as the only place in the international system where they have equal say with rich countries on the economic and development issues of greatest concern to them. Because they see the UN as "their" organization, they react strongly to anything that looks like a threat to their voice in determining the UN's development role or to any effort to curtail that role.

A group of four leading candidates for permanent Security Council seats—Japan, Germany, India, and Brazil—was concerned primarily with getting those seats.

But, as has frequently been the case in efforts at UN reform, inept diplomacy and deliberate obstructionism skewered any chance for a grand bargain. Instead of a long stride forward into global governance for the twenty-first century, the summit took only baby steps forward. The world's leaders managed only piecemeal agreements, and even in those areas decisions on many of the hard details were deferred.

Security Council expansion fell by the wayside, with the four leading contenders for new permanent seats undermined by regional rivalries and the general lack of willingness on the part of other states to commit political capital to the issue. On development, the summit's outcome document merely reaffirmed previous agreements. Terrorism was roundly condemned but remained undefined.

But the summit did manage to agree to the creation of the Peacebuilding Commission, the establishment of the new Human Rights Council, new resources for oversight of the Secretariat, and support for an effort to think anew about systemwide coherence. It also, surprisingly, accepted language asserting that governments that fail to meet their "responsibility to protect" their citizens from such basic threats as genocide risk surrendering their cherished sovereignty to an international community that may choose to act on behalf of those citizens.

Current Status of Reforms

Annan's efforts to push management reform have fallen afoul of perceptions among developing country representatives that he is merely a front for the U.S. agenda—a perception not widely shared in the United States. In addition, because Annan's term as secretary-general finishes at the end of 2006, he is treated as a lame duck, unable to cut deals on a package of reforms. The debate over an agreed definition of terrorism is stuck in the General Assembly's Sixth Committee, victim of intra-UN politicking. Although hopes for Security Council reform spring eternal, there is little realistic prospect for agreement in the near future. The Peacebuilding Commission has been authorized. However, its membership is supposed to be determined in part by the Economic and Social Council (ECOSOC) and the General Assembly, both of which have dragged their feet in naming their representatives to the organizing committee. The new Human Rights Council exists, with a new membership that excludes some of the most objectionable human rights violators, although it still includes several countries with questionable human rights records.

Management reform remains a most contentious issue. In December 2005 several of the countries that pay the bulk of the UN's assessed budget pushed through a proposal that appropriated only enough funding to carry the UN through June 2006, with the budget for the remainder of the year to be contingent on adequate progress on management reform. Left undefined was what would constitute "adequate" progress. By late June 2006, the United States was arguing that the progress to date had been inadequate, but it found little support among other member states. As of July, the United States had lifted its opposition to continued funding of the UN budget, and the General Assembly enacted a modest package of management reform measures.

In addition, the secretary-general has convened yet another high-level panel, this one meant "to explore how the UN system could work more coherently and effectively across the world in the areas of development, humanitarian assistance and the environment." The coherence panel is unusual if not unprecedented in that its three co-chairs are not mere luminaries but are sittings heads of government: Prime Minister Shaukat Azia of Pakistan; Prime Minister Luisa Dias Diogo of Mozambique; and Prime Minister Jens Stoltenberg of Norway. Nonetheless, the G-77 has reacted less than enthusiastically. One ambassador from a leading developing country was quoted as saying, "Under the guise of achieving greater efficiency and avoiding duplication, I believe the developed countries want to devoid the UN of its role in development, and leave it to deal only with security, post-conflict, humanitarian and environment issues."

Where Next?

The year 2005 saw the failure of the hoped-for "grand bargain" for the United Nations. It was followed in 2006 by minor progress in a handful of areas but with few prospects for any real breakthroughs. Having missed one major opportunity to revitalize the flawed but still essential United Nations and transform it into the kind of organization needed to deal with the realities of the twenty-first century, the world now must figure out how to do better. The first step is to assign responsibility where it truly belongs: overwhelmingly with the member countries, particularly the world's economically and militarily dominant powers. Blaming "the UN" (usually meaning the Secretariat) for the scandals and failures of the world body is like blaming a concert hall's management for a poor performance. While there is an institutional responsibility to make sure that the roof does not leak and the ticket-sellers are not pocketing the proceeds, it is the musicians who have to perform. At the UN, the players are prone to break into fistfights at concert time—if they show up at all.

The member countries have never invested the financial and human resources needed to enable the UN to carry out the many mandates that they impose on it. Many act like absentee landlords, pocketing rents in the form of jobs for a handful of their nationals but otherwise largely ignoring the institution. A few hard-core opponents of reform—insiders point to the representatives of Syria, Pakistan, Venezuela, Cuba, Egypt, and Iran—actively subvert attempts to make the UN function efficiently and effectively. The United States, where Congress goes into periodic fits of rage over revelations of misdeeds such as the oil-for-food scandal, has only fitfully paid attention or pushed the executive branch to engage in the long-term, patient diplomacy needed to build consensus for meaningful change.

What has been missing from the multitude of efforts to reform the UN is a workable bargaining venue in which states could look at the system as a whole, cut the deals needed for a broadly acceptable package that leaves everyone better off, and provide the sustained political muscle to prevent the usual obstructionists from destroying the package within the UN itself. The G-20 countries have the breadth of representation, financial capacity, and influence to underpin a realistic process of negotiating trade-offs, and they could attempt to formulate a package through their representatives at the UN. Alternatively, they could try to take negotiations outside the UN system, try to achieve coherence, and then sell a more "rational" package back to the broader UN membership. But that proposal raises many questions about the substance of the package of issues, the connection with other international (and regional) bodies, and the decisionmaking process.

A compelling package—or a process to put it together—is far from becoming a reality. However, both the need for such a package and the impediments to past efforts have been recognized. For those internationalists committed to moving ahead, we close with the kinds of questions that need to be addressed skillfully in order to develop solutions that will reinvigorate the multilateral system—and keep nations buying into it rather than seeking excuses to opt out.

—Given that the G-20 leaders (the L-20) themselves are not likely to develop a proposed package, serving instead to endorse something developed elsewhere, who should take on the role of developing the next "grand bargain"? Should it be one large package, or should it be seen as a series of agreements staged over many years?

—The L-20 includes only large countries. What process could ensure that the interests of small countries are adequately represented?

—What issues should be included in the package? Only those pertinent to the developing countries, given that the Security Council already has a small group (the P-5) addressing security issues?

—How should the interests, roles, and capabilities of regional organizations be taken into account in formulating an agenda for UN reform?

All nations have a stake in fully investing themselves in the effort to find viable answers to those questions.

Notes

1. *A More Secure World: Our Shared Responsibility,* Report of the Secretary-General's High-Level Panel on Threats, Challenges, and Change (United Nations, 2004), p. 3.

2. Ibid., p. 9.

3. Roberta Cohen. "No Quick Fix for Darfur," *Northwestern Journal for International Affairs* 8 (Spring 2006).

4. NATO, "NATO-ISAF Expands to Southern Afghanistan," press release, July 31, 2006.

5. Testimony by Henry A. Crumpton, "Reviewing the State Department's Annual Report on Terrorism," House Committee on International Relations, Subcommittee on International Terrorism and Nonproliferation, 109 Cong. 2 sess., May 11, 2006.

6. "America's Image Slips, but Allies Share U.S. Concerns over Iran, Hamas," *Pew Global Attitudes Project* (Washington: Pew Research Center, June 13, 2006).

PART **II**

Global Governance Reform

5

Summit Reform:
Toward an L-20

JOHANNES F. LINN AND COLIN I. BRADFORD JR.

The United Nations summit of September 2005 was conceived with lofty expectations for strengthening the system of global governance by reforming and strengthening the UN. However, little was achieved. That failure has left unanswered the challenge of creating a more legitimate—that is, more effective and inclusive—system of global governance than currently exists.

The many global tasks confronting world political leaders today—whether the stalemate of global trade negotiations, the threat of avian flu, the struggle over Iran's plans for a nuclear program, or the fight against global poverty—cannot be solved by yesterday's institutions. Such tasks demand new approaches to global governance that are more inclusive and representative and thus more effective.

The G-8 summit offers an especially glaring example of a global institution that is in need of reform. While it conceives of itself as the apex of global consultation and decisionmaking, the G-8 is a forum of the eight industrialized countries that were the dominant powers of the mid-twentieth century. By excluding the major emerging powers of the twenty-first century, it has become increasingly ineffective, unrepresentative, and illegitimate. The inter-

This chapter is an updated version of the authors' "Pragmatic Reform of Global Governance: Creating an L-20 Summit Forum," Brookings Policy Brief 152 (April 2006).

ests of the international community, including those of the United States, are best served by increasing the inclusiveness and effectiveness of the global steering process rather than sticking with the obsolete, overly formalized, and unrepresentative G-8.

This chapter explores alternatives that could be considered in creating a more inclusive summit architecture. One pragmatic solution, and one that we think may well be most appropriate, is for the G-8 to make room for and eventually give way to an expanded summit—a "Leaders' 20" (or "L-20"), comprising the leaders of the world's twenty key countries—as the new forum of global negotiation and decisionmaking. But other options for enlarging the summit also should be considered, since they may be more politically feasible at any given time. To make a real difference, however, a significant change from the current exclusive approach is necessary to ensure that the major emerging market economies are brought "into the tent" and thus encouraged to contribute constructively to the solution of global issues and share the burden of challenges that the old industrial countries cannot expect to solve on their own.

The Challenge of Global Governance Reform

The limitations of the current global governance institutions are manifold and manifest, in addition to the weaknesses inherent in the G-8 summit framework already mentioned. The UN decisionmaking processes are cumbersome, mostly ineffective, and hard to change. The international financial institutions (IFIs) have specific operational mandates and do not provide summit-level forums for addressing overarching global issues. And they face their own intractable issues of legitimacy. Other global organizations and forums are fragmented and focused on single issues; they do not function as a summit-level mechanism for addressing multiple issues in a cross-cutting and integrative manner.

Many reform proposals have addressed the weaknesses in global governance. They have included ideas to improve decisionmaking at the UN—for example, by setting up a special security council that would provide guidance on global socioeconomic and environmental issues. Others have pushed for reform of the IFIs, proposing, for example, to upgrade their governing bodies to summit-level forums. There also has been some debate on various ideas for reforming the G-8 summits. From our perspective, in view of the record of failed efforts to reform the UN and the IFIs, the last avenue—reform of the G-8—represents the best opportunity in the foreseeable future to advance global governance reform in a pragmatic and meaningful manner; indeed, it is an important first step toward reforming the other global institutions as well.

The Challenges Facing the G-7/8 and the G-20

The G-7, predecessor of the G-8, was formed in 1977 as a forum in which the leaders of the major Western industrial economies could gather to deal with economic imbalances among members of the group. During the days of the cold war, the G-7 also saw itself as a club of democracies intent on countering the threat of Soviet power and expansionism. After the collapse of the Soviet Union and the end of the cold war, the president of Russia was invited to attend G-7 meetings. In 1998 Russia joined as a full member of what then became the annual G-8 summit. Over the years the leaders of selected non-G-8 countries have been invited to join parts of the G-8 summits on an ad hoc and part-time basis in an effort to increase the reach and inclusiveness of the annual summit events.

Although Russia was admitted to the G-8, the G-7 finance ministers and central bank governors, who had been meeting between the annual G-7 summits, did not invite Russia to join them. Instead, in 1999, in the wake of the 1997–98 global financial crises, the G-7 finance ministers set up a new finance forum, the G-20, which includes the major emerging market economies (see figure 5-1). As a result, what is in effect a two-track global steering mechanism is now in place, with a "finance" track (the G-7/G-20) and a "leader" track (the G-8). In view of that development, we will refer to the G-7/G-20 as the F-7/F-20 and to the G-8 as the L-8 in the remainder of this chapter.[1]

The F-20 is geographically and culturally diverse. Representing two-thirds of the global population and about 90 percent of the global economy, it is broadly inclusive. The emerging market economy members of the F-20 have become fully engaged, with China chairing the F-20 in 2005, as India and Mexico did in earlier years. Most observers credit the F-20 with a productive track record in dealing with important global financial issues.

At the same time, the legitimacy of the L-8 has been undermined by two incongruent trends: on one hand, the L-8 summits have increasingly turned from issues of internal group coordination to issues of broad global economic and political significance, with the L-8 arrogating to itself the role of de facto global steering committee. On the other hand, the rapid shifts in demographic and economic weight from global "North" to "South" have made the

Figure 5-1. *The G-20 Membership*

INDUSTRIALIZED ECONOMIES	DEVELOPING ECONOMIES
Australia	Argentina
Canada	Brazil
France	China
Germany	India
Italy	Indonesia
Japan	South Korea
Russia	Mexico
United Kingdom	Saudi Arabia
United States	South Africa
European Union	Turkey

Source: Group of Twenty (www.g20.org).

L-8 more and more unrepresentative. Moreover, L-8 summits have been characterized as increasingly formalized and lacking real impact in addressing major global challenges.[2]

There have been frequent calls for improvements in the two tracks of the global steering mechanism. Some have called for further strengthening of the finance track. Others have called for a broadening of the leader track. We believe that setting up an L-20 in tandem with the F-20 is an appropriate and pragmatic route to follow for quick and meaningful progress in global governance reform. However, other options for an expanded, more inclusive summit forum also are possible, as discussed below.

Proposal for an L-20 Summit Forum

There are many good reasons for setting up an L-20 summit forum. First, there is the need for an effective, representative, and legitimate global steering process to address global challenges. An L-20, while by no means perfect, would go a long way toward achieving the goal of broad representativeness. Second, an L-20 would draw in the major emerging market economies so that they share responsibility for the solution of global issues that cannot be resolved without their constructive engagement. Third, global challenges increasingly cut across individual agencies and sectorial forums; hence an integrated view is needed at the leader level that cuts across ministerial, sectorial, and agency lines. Fourth, reform of other global institutions (the UN, IFIs, and so forth) is important, but reform efforts are not likely to progress quickly. Finally, the F-20 already exists at the ministerial level, albeit with a narrow finance focus; an L-20 can be created by simple invitation, without complex legal action and without opening up a Pandora's box of arguments over who is in and who is out of the group. An L-20, once established, could become an effective forum to push ahead reform in other global institutions.

Key Questions for L-8 Summit Reform

Five questions need to be addressed in arguing for L-8 summit reform. We focus here on the challenges related specifically to implementing an L-20, but a similar set of questions would have to be addressed when considering other options for enlarging the G-8.

What would be the role of the L-20 summit?

A common question is whether an L-20 would function as a global steering mechanism or as forum for discussion and networking among major global players. Our answer is that it should and would function in both capacities, depending on the subject under consideration. When consensus on needed actions can be reached among L-20 members, it should be translated into directives to their representatives at the international and national organizations responsible for implementation in the areas on which agreement has been reached. For areas on which consensus cannot be reached, an L-20 would serve as a useful forum for exchanging views and narrowing differences, for building coalitions, and for searching for compromises and trade-offs across different issues.

Would an L-20 be a legitimate global governance forum?

The legitimacy of a governance body derives from a combination of representativeness and effectiveness, but unfortunately there is an inevitable tension between the two. As the number of participants increases, a summit becomes more representative of the world community, yet its effectiveness as a deliberative and decisionmaking body is likely to decline. However, it is important to remember that the effectiveness of implementation also matters. If a forum achieves consensus, but the key actors needed to implement the agreed action are not at the table, chances are that the action will not be effectively implemented. While there are no hard-and-fast rules for determining the optimum size, we believe that a group of twenty represents an acceptable trade-off among objectives and conveys an appropriate degree of legitimacy. Legitimacy could be further enhanced if ways were found to have some (or all) participants speak not only for themselves but also on behalf of groups of nonrepresented countries by, for example, bringing to the table the views of regional bodies, such as the African Union.

What substantive areas would an L-20 summit address?

This is a very common question, rightly asked. One answer is that any topic of global significance suitable for the L-8 would also be appropriate for the L-20. Another answer is that an L-20 would make up its own agenda in response to pressures from evolving global issues. While both answers are justified, it nevertheless is useful to point to some specific areas in which a broadly representative summit process could help resolve important global issues.

In our view there is no dearth of topics of critical global significance and urgency that an enhanced summit forum could and should address. One of them is the threat of global epidemics, in particular the threat of avian flu. Another area of immediate urgency is the question of how to deal with Iran's nuclear plans. Other possible summit topics would be how to mobilize global attention and support for the war on global poverty, in particular for achievement of the Millennium Development Goals; how to deal with the current global energy crunch; how to address global environmental threats, such as global warming; how to develop strategies for preparedness and response to major natural disasters such as the tsunamis, hurricanes, and earthquakes that struck in 2005; and how to address global security issues, including weapons of mass destruction, terrorism, and failed states. Finally, an L-20 summit would be an excellent forum for seeking agreement on long-elusive reforms of existing international institutions (especially reform of the UN and the IFIs). These are all global issues, not restricted to the industrial countries of the twentieth century. There is no summit-level forum now for dealing with these problems, and that void at the apex weakens the world's capacity to manage itself in the twenty-first century.

Why an L-20 rather than other summit options?

Much of the discussion on the topic of summit reform revolves around the membership and constellation of the summit framework. We summarize the most commonly considered options in figure 5-2. They start with the status quo (an F-7 and F-20 on the finance track and the L-8 on the leader track). A minimal but significant reform option would be to add China to the L-8, or perhaps even Brazil, China, India, and South Africa, which together with Russia make up the so-called BRICS. While that certainly would represent progress, we believe that a geographically, economically, and demographically more inclusive approach is appropriate and feasible.[3]

Figure 5-2. *Options for Summit Reform*

1. F-7/L-8 + F-20[a]
2. F-7/L-9 + F-20 (add China to L-8)
3. F-7/L-12 + F-20 (add BRICS to L-7)
4. F-7/L-8 + F-20 / L-20
5. F-7 + F-20/L-20
6. F-20/L-20
7. F-16/L-16 (one seat for EU)
8. Variable geometry: L (X + Y), where X is the permanent core and Y varies depending on topic matter

a. F = ministers of finance; L = leaders (summit).

Taking the incremental approach of adding members to a logical but prag-matic conclusion would mean establishing an L-20, either in addition to the L-8 (option 4 in figure 5-2) or, more radically, also eliminating the L-8 or F-7 or both. Under the principle of a "hard budget constraint for institu-tions"—that is, whenever a new institution is added, an existing one is abolished—the replacement rather than additional summit option would be recommended, even though it may not be realistic in the near term since the current L-8 members are likely to be unwilling to give up that forum for now.

Another radical step would be to merge the five EU "chairs" in the sum-mits into one chair. That would have the benefit of reducing the number of chairs or freeing up some chairs for other significant countries excluded from the F-20/L-20. Such a step is not likely to be acceptable to the EU members in the foreseeable future, especially since the EU constitution has been put on ice.[4]

Other options could also be considered if a radical departure from the current summit framework is thought to be desirable and feasible. Some have proposed narrowing the summit membership further in the interest of effi-ciency and congruity of interest (for example, an L-2 for the EU and the United States; an L-3 for the EU, Japan, and the United States; or an L-4, which would add China to an L-3).[5] We believe that narrowing the member-ship base is entirely a move in the wrong direction. Others have suggested a "variable geometry" summit framework. This approach would start with a core of summit members (for example, the L-12, consisting of the L-8 members plus Brazil, China, India, and South Africa) and then add a different set of additional countries, subject to some maximum number (say seven, for a total of no more than twenty) depending on the summit topic. For example, for a summit on trade, a group of the seven countries that are most critical for reaching agreement could be added, while for a summit on the avian flu a different set of countries would be involved, presumably those most critical to its worldwide control. The variable geometry approach has much intuitive appeal, since it would bring to the table a limited number of the most appropriate countries and over time would be more inclusive than, say, a single L-20 forum. The main problem would likely be the difficulty of agreeing on which country is in and which is out for each topic and managing the process of multiple summit membership tracks for different topics. The non-core members would also be likely to be regarded as second class since they would not be permanent participants.

After wide consultations with officials in the F-20 countries, we have concluded that the more radical options shown in figure 5-2 are currently not realistic in terms of likely acceptance by key participants, while other options (those that would involve narrowing the scope of membership) go in the wrong direction. Proceeding incrementally, by first creating an L-20 and then moving to some of the more radical solutions (reducing the number of summit forums and consolidating the EU chairs) appears to us both a desirable and pragmatic option for progressively reforming a key element of the global governance structure. Alternatively, one might want to build up gradually to a variable geometry approach, choosing topics and groups of countries on a more ad hoc basis to respond to the pressing global issues of the day. That approach may be more acceptable at the moment to the members of the L-8 and hence have a greater chance of moving forward.

How would an L-20 be implemented?

Implementation of any new, expanded summit forum would present new challenges. First among them would be how to ensure informality of discourse among the leaders in a larger group when doing so already is a problem for the smaller group of the L-8. That could be achieved by getting leaders to meet, at least for part of the summits, in an informal setting without their retinues of ministers and other assistants. Second would be how to organize the presidency of the summit. One option would be to adopt the current F-20 rotating "troika" approach, wherein the immediate past and future presidents form a troika with the current chair in setting the agenda and monitoring progress. Third would be how to organize the function of the secretariat. It could be informal, along the lines of the current summits, or a formal, standing secretariat could be established, possibly at an existing institution such as the Organization for Economic Cooperation and Development, the United Nations Development Program, or the World Bank. Fourth would be whether to continue to include a "sherpa" process, as for the current summits.[6] Even with a formal secretariat, that would seem appropriate, and for specific areas such as trade, health, and the environment, a consultative process led by ministers and tasked with the technical and political preparation of the summits could be envisaged. Finally would be the question of what links, formal or informal, would exist to other global institutions (the UN, the IFIs, the WTO, the WHO, and so forth). One option is to continue the practice of inviting the UN secretary-general and the heads of IFIs to the summits. In addition, links could be established or maintained at the ministerial level by the sherpas and by the secretariat, if one is created.

Conclusion

The questions raised in this chapter are important, and they deserve to be considered carefully by the main stakeholders in the global governance debate. However, we also believe that the sooner a decision is made to expand the current, overly restricted and obsolete L-8 summit group the better. In our view the L-8 is unable to serve as a legitimate global governance forum. That will become increasingly and ever more painfully obvious as time progresses. The earlier the current membership of the L-8 moves on summit reform, the better. In our view the proposed L-20 offers a ready-made, pragmatic option for moving forward quickly, visibly, and effectively with the global governance reform agenda. Alternatives could and should be considered, and questions of purpose, representation, effectiveness, and legitimacy and of substantive focus and implementation should be explored. But bearing in mind that summit reform can be a first step to more global governance change down the road, it would be better to move sooner rather than later on creating a more inclusive global summit framework.

There is little doubt that no such change will occur unless the United States participates actively in the process of deliberating and exploring alternatives and then agrees to a new summit format. In April 2004 we argued that summit reform is in the U.S. national interest but noted that it would entail significant shifts in U.S. foreign policy—from Atlanticism to globalism, from unilateralism to multilateralism, and from leadership by power to leadership by persuasion and inclusion.[7] That remains the case today. Perhaps the chances that the United States will consider summit reform seriously are somewhat better today than they were two years ago since the current administration now appears more willing than it was previously to consider multilateral organizations and forums as relevant instruments for its global agenda and ready to give greater attention to considering the appropriate role of emerging economies in multilateral institutions.[8] We have no doubt that U.S. global interests are best served by increasing the inclusiveness and effectiveness of the summits, rather than sticking with the L-8, which is now obsolete, overly formalized, and unrepresentative.

Notes

1. The G-7 finance ministers' meeting was hosted and joined by Russia in St. Petersburg in June 2006, while Russia chaired the G-8. Whether this sets a pattern for future years remains to be seen. In any case, it appears that the finance ministers want to maintain their forum, and hence it helps to clarify their meetings as F-7, F-8, or F-20 meetings.

2. See Colin I. Bradford Jr. and Johannes F. Linn, "Global Economic Governance at a Crossroads: Replacing the G-7 with the G-20," Brookings Policy Brief 131, April 2004.

3. Option 3 in figure 5-2, under which the L-8 is augmented by adding Brazil, China, India, and South Africa, would leave the Middle East entirely out of the summit forum. An L-8+5, which adds Brazil, China, India, Mexico, and South Africa (also sometimes referred to as BRICSM) already exists for global environmental deliberations and would provide a further widening of the summit framework. In his May 26, 2006, speech at Georgetown University in Washington, U.K. prime minister Tony Blair endorsed the G-8+5, which in his view "should be the norm" (www.number10.gov.uk/output/Page9549.asp).

4. The creation of a single chair for the EU members is, of course, also possible under other options.

5. In June 2006 the IMF announced the creation of a group consisting of China, the Eurozone, Japan, Saudi Arabia, and the United States to consider options for reducing global financial imbalances. While at the ministerial, not the summit level, this particular group (which we could refer to as F-5) indicates some of the innovative approaches now being experimented with.

6. "Sherpas" are the high-level officials from member governments who prepare the summit or ministerial-level meetings in close coordination with each other.

7. In "Global Economic Governance at a Crossroads."

8. U.S. support for proposals to increase the shares of emerging market economies in the IMF is a case in point.

6

The Bank-Fund Ministerial Committees

JACK BOORMAN AND ALEX SHAKOW

T wo ministerial committees meet at the annual spring and fall meetings of the board of governors of the International Monetary Fund (IMF) and of the World Bank to provide guidance to each institution and to chart a course for the international community in dealing with international monetary issues and development problems. The International Monetary and Financial Committee (IMFC) of the IMF focuses primarily on the international monetary system and matters of direct relevance to the fund, whereas the Development Committee, a joint committee of the bank and the IMF, gives priority to developing countries and development challenges, including resource needs. Both committees consist of twenty-four ministers from industrial and developing countries. These committees present examples of global governance at the international institutional level that are highly relevant not only for issues that are specifically related to reform of individual international institutions but also for more general global governance issues as well.

The sections of this chapter that precede the heading "The Role of the Development Committee in Global Governance" (p. 93) were written by Jack Boorman; subsequent sections were written by Alex Shakow.

The IMFC: Its Origin and Future

The work of the IMF governing bodies—the board of governors, the IMFC, and the executive board—is not widely understood. Twice each year, the International Monetary and Financial Committee meets and issues a communiqué summarizing the views of the participants on a number of issues confronting the international monetary system, the global economy, and the IMF. The range of topics covers the current state of the world economy and its prospects; economic and financial vulnerabilities that may be considered global or regional; policy issues under discussion in the fund; global initiatives in which the fund may be involved; and administrative or even certain personnel issues facing the institution. The communiqué, which generally receives close attention in the financial press, is likely to get only passing attention in the broader press and media. However, it receives close scrutiny within the IMF itself and often, depending on the issues addressed, within other institutions and governments. But what is the IMFC? What is its role and mandate? Who are its members and what power or authority does it possess? It is always useful to begin with some history.

Role and Mandate

Until August 1971, the par value system of exchange rates that had been established with the creation of the IMF had as its centerpiece a fixed value of the U.S. dollar defined in terms of gold, values of other currencies set in relation to the dollar, and free conversion of official dollar holdings into gold. The connection between the dollar and gold was severed in August 1971 as continuing pressure on the U.S. balance of payments led to fear of an adjustment in the dollar/gold relationship and hence to an increase in conversions of official dollar holdings into gold. In December 1971, under the Smithsonian Agreement, new exchange rate relationships were established, leading to a de facto devaluation of the U.S. dollar and introducing somewhat wider bands around the new exchange rates. However, that arrangement also failed in a relatively short time.

The turmoil in the international monetary system led to the formation in July 1972 of a group formally known as the Committee of the Board of Governors on Reform of the International Monetary System and Related Matters and informally known as the Committee of Twenty (C-20). The C-20 comprised ministers from each of the twenty constituencies that, at that time, had directors on the IMF's executive board. In recognition of the fact that the issues that the committee was to address were political as well as economic, it was convened at the ministerial level. At the same time, however, it was referred to as "ad hoc" because it was not intended to be a permanent body of the IMF. In October 1974 the C-20 submitted its Outline of Reform to the board of governors and then ceased to exist. However, the C-20 had stated, inter alia, that "it would be desirable to establish by amendment of the Articles of Agreement a permanent and representative Council." Pending the establishment of such a council, it was decided to establish immediately "an Interim Committee of the Board of Governors on The International Monetary System with an advisory role." Among the motives for establishing the Interim Committee (IC), pending action on a council, were the fact that although the ad hoc C-20 was seen to have been useful, its work was considered unfinished; the clear realization that reform would be evolutionary and would not be accomplished quickly; and finally, the belief that a permanent body would be more helpful than an ad hoc committee in strengthening the IMF—for example, by allowing for direct political representation of the membership.

The Outline of Reform did not propose a new international monetary or exchange rate system, partly because of the uncertainties that then prevailed, including those related to the U.S. economy, which were in part due to the Vietnam war; the oil crisis, triggered by the quadrupling of oil prices in 1973–74; surging inflation and "stagflation" in industrial countries; large imbalances in the balance of payments of many member countries; and the associated huge recycling of oil revenue through commercial banks, which was creating unprecedented levels of cross-border debt.

The immediate steps taken to deal with the new world of floating exchange rates led to the second amendment of the Articles of Agreement, which was adopted by the board of governors in April 1976 and went into effect in April 1978. The second amendment essentially legalized floating exchange rates, giving members the right to establish exchange rate regimes of their choice; called on the IMF to exercise "firm surveillance" over exchange rates and on members to cooperate with the fund in that effort; modified the role of gold, reserve currencies, and special drawing rights (SDRs); and, as noted, gave the board of governors the authority to establish a council (with the approval of members holding at least 85 percent of the total voting power in the fund). Interestingly, in addition to managing and adapting the international monetary system, the council was to "review developments in the transfer of real resources to developing countries," one of the rationales for creating the Development Committee and the reason why it was created as a joint committee of the World Bank and the IMF.

The Interim Committee was to guide the IMF in fulfilling its new responsibilities under the second amendment. In the view of most observers, the Interim Committee has performed a useful function. Among other things, it played a key role in formulating and securing agreement on the second amendment; it helped deal with the oil crisis of the 1970s—for example, by establishing an oil facility in the fund to assist oil-importing countries in financing and adjusting to higher oil prices; it was instrumental in formulating an agreement on the sale of gold that included using some of the proceeds of those sales for distribution to the membership and for establishment of a trust fund for loans to the poorer countries; it supported the approach taken to dealing with the debt crisis of the 1980s, including the bailing-in of commercial banks and, ultimately, the Brady plan; it helped place the IMF in a key role in dealing with the transition economies in the early 1990s; and it helped deal with the emerging markets crises of the mid- and late 1990s.

Forces for Change

However, there were some failures as well. For example, the Interim Committee failed to find agreement on an allocation of SDRs to new members—mostly the transition economies that had joined the IMF in the early 1990s—at the annual meetings in Madrid in 1994. Interestingly, some see an element of success in that event, as it reflected the new power of the developing countries in the committee to block something that they did not support.

Notwithstanding the proven usefulness of the Interim Committee, some thought the transition from an interim committee to a council was overdue. After all, the Interim Committee itself was not intended to be a permanent body; it was to be replaced by a council as recommended in the final report of the C-20 and as provided for in article XII of the Articles of Agreement as amended in 1978. The council would have decisionmaking authority, unlike the C-20 and the Interim Committee, which were only advisory. The council would sit between the executive board and the board of governors (the latter comprising representatives of all 184 members), but it would be more like a surrogate for the board of governors in supervising the management and adaptation of the international monetary system and of the fund as the key institution in that system. It would be the forum for decisionmaking regarding issues such as quotas, SDR allocations, further amendments to the Articles of Agreement, and other important matters.

One of those who thought that the time had come for the establishment of a council was Michel Camdessus, who had been the managing director of the IMF during 1987–2000. Camdessus saw the need for a mechanism to ensure that the general public understood the fund's accountability more clearly.

The IMF is accountable and responsible to its member governments; all of its decisions are approved by its executive board, made up of twenty-four members representing all 184 member countries. The member governments, voting through the executive board, control the fund and are responsible for its decisions. However, there is a telling quote in a speech that Camdessus gave to the Council on Foreign Relations around the time of his departure as managing director in February 2000. Speaking on this issue, he noted that "the problem is not that we are not accountable but that we are not seen to be accountable, and that some member governments from time to time find it convenient not to express their public support for actions they have supported in the Executive Board."[1]

That appeared to be a candid expression of frustration with the fact that some governments seemed publicly to be second guessing or even distancing themselves from some of the more controversial operations of the fund, especially in Russia and in some of the Asian crisis countries. Camdessus went on to say that

> it is important to ensure that the IMF is seen far more visibly to have the legitimate political support of our shareholders. One reform that I have recently supported would respond to this problem. It would entail transforming the IMF's advisory ministerial committee into a decision-making council for the major strategic orientations of the world economy. Far from leading to an undue politicization of the IMF, this would simply, in the eyes of the public, place responsibility squarely where it already rests.

But Camdessus did not succeed in that effort. However, he was successful in transforming the Interim Committee into the International Monetary and Financial Committee in September 1999—a significant step toward creating a permanent body, although it was still an advisory rather than a decision-making group. One of the provisions introduced to strengthen the role of the IMFC was to hold deputy-level meetings to help prepare for the ministerial meeting of the IMFC itself—something now routine but still controversial in some quarters.[2]

Facing the Future

Given the experience to date with the IMFC, it is worth asking whether it is up to the task assigned to it. That question might be broken into two parts:

first, does the IMFC effectively guide the institution, the IMF, in carrying out its responsibilities; second, does it play the role that it should in managing the global monetary system?

On the first question, the IMFC usually has been given good marks. Its record is generally good on issues such as guiding the IMF's response to crises, ensuring that the fund evolves in terms of the financial facilities that it maintains to assist members, and helping to ensure that the "architecture" of the international system keeps up with the increasing complexity of the globalized economy—all the work on standards, codes, and so forth. Similarly, the way in which the IMFC—often in collaboration with the Development Committee—has guided the fund's executive board and management on issues specific to low-income countries has generally been successful, sometimes in the face of extremely challenging legal and financial issues, including the design and funding of the recent Multilateral Debt Relief Initiative (MDRI).

With respect to the second question, however, many critics today say that the IMF is not doing as much as it should to confront the very large and growing imbalances in the global financial system. That is the foremost responsibility of the IMF in conducting "firm surveillance" over the exchange rate and the related macroeconomic policies of all of its member countries. Given the persistence of the imbalances, one is indeed tempted to question the IMFC's effectiveness in this area.[3]

But the issue can be tackled only by broadening the question: is the international community in general, including the IMFC, well organized to address such problems? There should be no question that the IMF is first and foremost responsible for providing the analytic basis for the assessment of such issues. That is done through surveillance of the policies of individual countries and assessment of the global implications of those policies. The latter is conducted primarily in the context of producing two publications, the *World Economic Outlook* and the *Global Financial Stability Report*. But when it comes time to encourage action by countries to take the needed corrective policy measures, are the IMF and the IMFC up to the task? That is a big question that can be answered only in the context of an examination of all the other bodies that play a role in this domain. It goes to the basic question of surveillance in the international community—How does power and representation in the IMF affect the capacity of the institution to conduct effective surveillance?—and to the role of other bodies like the G-8, G-20, or other "Gs" as agenda-setting bodies for the international institutions and, at times, as forums for seeking agreement on policies that cut across countries, including exchange rate and other economic and financial policies.

The crucial question is whether the current configurations of such groups make sense; are they optimally designed to deal effectively with the economic and financial challenges confronting the global economy? And do these groups relate effectively to the IMFC? These issues are taken up in chapters 1 and 9 of this volume.

The Role of the Development Committee in Global Governance

The Development Committee was created through joint resolutions approved by the boards of governors of the World Bank and the IMF on October 2, 1974. The official name of the committee is the Joint Ministerial Committee of the Boards of Governors of the Bank and the Fund on the Transfer of Real Resources to Developing Countries. Thus, both the World Bank and the IMF are involved in this committee, while the Interim Committee, formed at the same time, is concerned only with IMF issues.

The Development Committee's formal mandate is to advise the boards of governors of the bank and the fund on critical development issues and on the financial resources required to promote economic development in developing countries.

Committee membership is based on the constituencies represented on the boards of the two institutions. Thus the committee has twenty-four members, and each constituency determines who serves as its representative on the committee and for how long. The process varies from group to group. Many constituencies that include a significant number of countries simply rotate their committee representative every year or two, while others maintain the same representative for several years. Most committee members are finance ministers, but there also have been ministers of development cooperation, ministers of the economy, and, in at least one instance, a minister of foreign affairs. Twenty-seven organizations currently have observer status on the Development Committee. However, as time is short and ministers value the opportunity to meet and talk with each other, there is little opportunity for observers to speak at the committee sessions, unless they are specifically invited to do so given their special expertise on a certain agenda topic. For example, the director general of the World Trade Organization (WTO) has made many appearances before the committee as part of an effort to enable powerful finance ministers to become better informed and add their weight to debates at home on trade issues.

While the chair of the Interim Committee—now the International Monetary and Finance Committee—has always been a European, the chair of the

Development Committee has always been from a developing country. The practice is not written into either of the joint resolutions; it is based on a mutual understanding that has existed since the committees were established. The Development Committee chair rotates from region to region, with terms of two years that can be extended to four by vote of the committee. The present chairperson, Alberto Carrasquilla, Colombia's finance minister, is the eighteenth minister to lead the committee and the sixth from Latin America. In another unwritten but understood principle, based on the desire to help ensure balance, the permanent executive secretary of the Development Committee—currently Kiyoshi Kodera of Japan—has always been from an industrialized country.

The Development Committee meets for several hours twice a year—during the fall World Bank and IMF annual meetings and each spring—and the meetings usually are preceded by a dinner or followed by a luncheon discussion restricted to members, the executive secretary, and the heads of the bank and the fund.

The committee's agenda is formally set by the members, but in practice it is normally proposed by the two institutions (particularly by the bank), occasionally modified to some extent by the two executive boards, agreed to by the committee chair, and issued to the committee. (In recent years a deputies' meeting has also met to discuss the agenda topics about ten days before the ministers' meeting; the value of this additional preparatory session is under review.) Given the committee's broad mandate and the participation of both the bank and the fund, agenda topics have ranged widely. Among the topics considered in recent meetings are debt, trade, global monitoring of the Millennium Development Goals (MDGs), HIV/AIDS, infrastructure, resource flows, energy, the environment, the voice and vote of developing countries in the bank and the fund, and so forth. The range of topics, of which this list is but a limited example, is much broader, of course, than that of the IMFC agenda, given its focus on IMF policy issues. The committee's consideration of these issues is usually based on papers that have been prepared by bank or IMF staff or both and that also have been reviewed by the board or boards before being sent to Development Committee members. Occasionally, papers prepared by observers—for example, by the chair of the Development Assistance Committee of the Organization for Economic Cooperation and Development on aid issues—serve as the basis for a useful discussion.

A communiqué is issued at the end of each meeting. To arrive at a text that members will be able to agree on in the short time available, bank executive directors usually meet for many hours two days before the meeting to go over a draft prepared by the executive secretary of the committee. This draft is based on executive directors' suggested revisions to an earlier draft that draws on suggestions made by relevant bank and fund staff and management.

Is the Development Committee a Good Model for Global Governance?

When the late Mahbub ul Haq first proposed establishing an economic security council, he suggested that its members be foreign ministers but later changed to finance ministers instead. The structure he proposed looked a great deal like the Development Committee, though it had only twenty members. While I do not believe that the Development Committee, as currently constituted, could become an economic security council, it has many attractive characteristics, although others considerably weaken its potential to play such a grand role.

Pros

The Development Committee's membership is truly representative—all 184 members of the World Bank and the IMF are represented through its twenty-four members, and any governments wishing to attend the committee's meetings may do so. Moreover, as its mandate encompasses both the bank and the fund, the membership includes powerful ministers of finance from both developed and developing countries. That factor has weighed heavily in the consistent rejection of the occasional suggestion that the committee should be a World Bank–only group, better paralleling the IMFC's role in the IMF. A major concern has been that finance ministers would drop out, leaving most developed countries represented by development agency heads whose influence and importance are normally much less than those of their finance colleagues.

Developing countries have a significant voice on the committee, if they choose to use it. The chairperson is from a developing country, so in the hands of an articulate and forceful minister, issues of importance to developing countries can receive balanced treatment. Moreover, if developing countries appoint to the committee representatives who are able to present their case with clarity and intelligence, they have every opportunity to make a significant impact on their peers from the richer and more developed countries. Of course, if strong appointments are not made, many useful opportunities will be missed.

Because there are a number of informal occasions to meet as well as formal plenary sessions at each committee meeting, it is quite possible in a short period of time for ministers to hear the views of their counterparts on significant issues. While some ministers still read formal statements at the plenary session, many are able to engage in more informal discussions on substantive topics. In addition, prepared statements are circulated in advance to all delegations, obviating the need for the actual oral presentation of long statements, as was the pattern until a decade ago. The highly restricted lunch and dinner meetings offer especially useful occasions for exchanging views across traditional regional lines or country groupings. The meetings are usually quite brief and focused, and they have the advantage of bank and fund staff support in preparing materials.

The committee can be instrumental in initiating important new policy directions. For example, in 1985 it was in the Development Committee that the Special Fund for Africa was created, and in 1996 it was at a committee lunch that James Wolfensohn, then the World Bank president, was convinced by the ministers around the table that the bank could no longer avoid participating in some form of debt rescheduling for the poorest countries. Soon thereafter, the Heavily Indebted Poor Country (HIPC) Initiative was born. In more recent years, the committee has become the focal point for follow-up on progress in achieving the Millennium Development Goals and the venue in which South Africa's Trevor Manuel has pushed (as committee chair) for greater attention to strengthening the "voice" of developing countries in the bank and the IMF. These are simply illustrations of some of the important ways that the committee has contributed to addressing critical issues.

The Development Committee's existence and the timing of its meetings, held on a regular, predictable schedule, have meant that it is a very helpful "action-forcing event." Once issues are on the agenda, the need to focus institutional attention, come to grips with the issues, complete paperwork, and prepare the ground in a timely fashion creates greater impetus to act than does simply preparing for a regular board meeting. For example, the need to report regularly on progress in implementing the HIPC debt initiative served to galvanize action in both the bank and the IMF. The committee's communiqué and discussions serve to pressure the World Bank to improve its own performance—and occasionally, as in the case of debt initiatives, to pressure the IMF as well. For example, for many years a number of governments were concerned that the bank was devoting inadequate attention to trade issues. In a number of Development Committee meetings, ministers pressured the bank to address that weakness, and ultimately the bank acted. Moreover, throughout the year executive directors appeal to a greater authority ("As Ministers said in the recent DC Communiqué, . . .") as a way to remind management of actions that need to be taken on themes expressed in the communiqué.

Cons

The Development Committee is not a decisionmaking body in the formal sense, but rather a consultative and advisory body to the boards of governors of the bank and the IMF. The committee has no enforcement mechanism, and its conclusions are reached by consensus, so its influence derives from members' willingness to back up their executive directors. Nonetheless, in practice the committee's communiqués reflect the views of the governors of the two institutions, the bosses of the executive directors; therefore the language of a communiqué can be perceived as a "decision" even though it may not be framed that way.

Some members do not take the Development Committee very seriously, but by and large they do attend the sessions—although about a decade ago, before various procedural reforms began to be implemented, they often did not. The degree to which the committee is viewed as useful depends heavily on whether members from the United States and other major powers attend, the quality of the discussion, the demonstrated interest of the bank president in the committee, and the usefulness and timeliness of the topics on the agenda and the discussion papers prepared on the agenda issues.

As noted above, each constituency decides how to manage its representation on the committee. That sometimes has perverse results. For example, several years ago, Nigeria—which, as the largest country in Africa, has a crucial role to play in international affairs—was just rejoining the global community as a positive and constructive force. It so happened that just at that time the smallest country in Africa, Lesotho, rotated into the Development Committee chair for that constituency based on a rotation system set up years before. While it is understandable that all twenty-two members of the constituency would like the chance to hold the chair, this rotation system weakens the value and effectiveness of the committee as a place for discussion of major issues with key interlocutors. Similarly, under current arrangements, Spain is often in the chair representing Mexico, Venezuela, and Central America, given the anomalous presence of a European country in that constituency. There are a number of other such unusual arrangements in the twenty-four constituencies represented.

Another problem is that Europe is overrepresented on the Development Committee. Nine of twenty-four chairs are currently held by European nations, and when Spain is in the chair for its constituency, the number rises to ten. Since votes and decisions are not taken in the committee, the preponderance of European voices is a problem primarily in that it limits the time and opportunities for other voices to be heard.

Developing country ministers are sometimes placed in awkward positions, which understandably constrains their willingness to speak up strongly on certain issues. Thus, if a minister of finance is to meet the day after the Development Committee meets with a fellow minister in search of support in an upcoming IMF discussion or on a bilateral aid arrangement, it is not surprising that the minister would be reluctant to possibly offend his colleague over a broader issue before the committee. That puts a premium on a minister's ability to be articulate, forceful, and courageous enough to raise such issues in a way that does not undermine future bilateral talks. The power disparity cannot be overcome easily, especially for ministers from the poorest and most aid-dependent countries.

There is a tendency for some constituencies to adopt the lowest-common-denominator position, given differing viewpoints within the often diverse constituencies. That contrasts with the situation in the G-20, for example, where each country represents itself rather than a group of countries.

Conclusion

Many improvements have been made over the last decade to make the Development Committee's meetings more interesting, effective, and useful. More can be done, of course, with respect to some of the issues raised in this chapter. For example, constituencies can be encouraged to ensure that key countries are in the chair representing them at Development Committee meetings. These and other steps should be pursued, but I would not ask too much of the committee, given the constraints noted above.

The conversion to a council of the sort proposed by Michel Camdessus would be difficult to accomplish, and I do not see that it is needed. How can decisions be enforced—without creating an economic security council, whose prospects do not seem promising? More realistically, a forum of the G-20 type could be utilized to provide guidance for action by bodies such as the Development Committee in their own domains.

In the end, the Development Committee's effectiveness depends in particular on how seriously the bank president and members—especially the

United States—wish to take it. When President Wolfensohn first arrived, he made many of the improvements in the committee's procedures possible because he saw the benefits of having an informal exchange of views with a representative group of the bank's governors twice a year. But it takes hard work to maintain that spirit. It is crucial to have an interesting agenda; well-prepared, short, and significant papers; and the enthusiastic leadership of the bank president as well as the support and encouragement of the IMF managing director. Under those circumstances the Development Committee can play an important role in guiding the bank—and to a lesser extent the IMF—and in helping to focus the international economic, financial, and development community on issues of great importance.

Notes

1. "An Agenda for the IMF at the Start of the 21st Century: Remarks by Michel Camdessus at the Council on Foreign Relations," Council on Foreign Relations, New York, February 1, 2000.

2. The convening of deputies has reduced somewhat the role of the executive board in guiding the agenda of IMFC meetings and in influencing the communiqués produced at the meetings.

3. The recent initiative of the managing director of the IMF to conduct multilateral consultations on the issue of the global imbalances will provide an important test of the capacity of the fund, including the IMFC, to better deal with such problems.

7

Global Health Governance

RONALD WALDMAN

The field of global health has changed dramatically and with almost startling rapidity over the past few decades. The changes have been sweeping, affecting its structure, content, and scope. Only thirty years ago the world was celebrating the total eradication of smallpox, a disease that had been a universal scourge for centuries and that now, or so it was thought, would disappear completely into the history books. At that time, no one had heard and few, if any, had conceived of the possibility of other viral pandemics becoming as blatantly and relentlessly threatening as have HIV/AIDS, Severe Acute Respiratory Syndrome (SARS), and avian influenza. Even smallpox, we learn, may not really have been eradicated—and biological warfare using it and other engineered pathogens is an unfortunate possibility. The world is a very different place now—countries and continents are far more linked in terms of trade, communications, and even national security.

Accompanying the sweeping changes in the public health landscape—even the name has changed, from international health to global health—has been the entry of new players and institutions, each rushing to fill a perceived gap or weakness in the global health architecture. As a result, the design of global health governance, as it exists today, is the product of chaotic, opportunistic growth. It has not been carefully planned or implemented. What some see as an appropriate action is seen by others as rash and ill-considered. Donors and recipients, rich countries and poor, bench scientists and workers in the field do not share the same priorities for funding or for action. Decisionmaking is done across a diffuse array of bilateral and multilateral organizations in both the private and public spheres. There are many who would lead the way, relatively few who are willing to follow.

Should there be a formal structure for global health governance, one that could rationalize the increased attention to the many facets of contemporary global public health, not to mention the increased financing that is directed toward them? It is hard to see how the world's priorities can be achieved without one. After all, six of the Millennium Development Goals, namely those that address poverty, child health, maternal health, major communicable diseases, the environment, and global partnerships (including those to provide access to drugs) are directly related to global public health issues. Yet, in the relatively uncoordinated and unregulated policy and funding environment that has come to characterize the field, some of those areas benefit from vastly increased (although still insufficient) attention and funding, while others struggle just to retain the very low level of priority that they traditionally have been accorded. A serious and coordinated effort is needed to ensure that steady progress toward achieving these goals is made.

The Peak of the Pyramid: WHO

The World Health Organization (WHO), a specialized technical agency of the United Nations, is the most prominent of the public sector global health institutions. Governance of WHO is wholly representative and democratic. Its executive board consists of thirty-four members, each of whom represents a member state. Members, usually ministers of health or their equivalent, are elected for three-year terms; there are no permanent members. The main function of the executive board is to develop, with the help of the 3,500-person staff, a biennial program of work and an accompanying budget; it then recommends the budget to the World Health Assembly for adoption.

The assembly is the major decisionmaking body of the organization, and it also is charged with responsibility for overseeing WHO's financial and technical policies. Inherently political, the assembly consists of representatives of the 192 current member states, each of which has a vote on the resolutions forwarded to it by the executive board.

The ability of WHO to provide legitimate and effective leadership in global public health is generally felt to be hampered by two factors. The first is the considerable power that is vested in its six regional offices. The problem is not with the offices themselves, but with the fact that regional directors are elected by the member states of their respective regions. Regional directors therefore tend to feel accountable to their member states, not to the director general, and that tendency has the effect of weakening the global authority of the organization. Politics, after all, is politics, and policies and decisions adopted for political reasons are not always technically sound.

The second factor is WHO's budget, which also poses problems. The organization's regular operating budget is determined by assessments imposed on the member states in a manner similar to that for the United Nations as a whole. The regular budget for the two-year period 2006–07 is on the order of $1 billion. The work of the organization, however, is driven in large part by "voluntary contributions" to WHO's programs. Those contributions come from donors among the member states who have a strong interest in supporting one or more programs that are consistent with their own priorities in global health. Voluntary contributions to WHO programs for 2006–07 are on the order of $2.2 billion, about twice the regular budget (about 70 percent of the total budget). Among the larger WHO programs, voluntary contributions account for 86 percent of the budget for communicable disease prevention and control, 94 percent of the HIV/AIDS budget, and 96 percent of the allocation for immunization and vaccine development. In contrast, external contributions account for "only" 43 percent of the much smaller program aimed at chronic, noncommunicable diseases and 47 percent of the program that addresses human resources for the health field. The bottom line is that as representative as WHO may be—and the argument can be made that, at least at the regional level, it may be too representative for a technical agency—its budget clearly is not under its own control and its principal areas of work are determined by its wealthier members.

Other Multilateral Agencies

Partly as a result of WHO's inability to provide consistently effective, decisive leadership on issues of health affecting all of its constituents and partly as a reflection of its lack of fiscal independence, a number of other multilateral organizations have taken it upon themselves to develop their own health mandates. For example, within the UN family of agencies alone, the United Nations Children's Fund (UNICEF), United Nations Population Fund (UNFPA), and the Food and Agriculture Organization/World Food Program

(FAO/WFP) have put increasing emphasis on the health and nutrition concerns of their specific constituencies. Although there are always at least nominal attempts at coordination with WHO and with each other, these agencies, with their own channels of accountability, regularly pursue independent, unlinked health initiatives.

While voluntary contributions to WHO represent part of the spending of donor countries, most, if not all, of them maintain their own bilateral programs. Some concentrate their spending on specific disease control programs that are of interest to them, while others seek, through various instruments, to contribute more generally to the strengthening of developing country health systems.

The biggest financial contributor to global health programs is the World Bank. The bank maintains a small network of health technicians and also has technical experts in public health in most of its regional divisions. Recently, there have been occasional calls for it to relinquish its technical expertise to other agencies, while maintaining or even increasing its financing of the global public health sector, but it is unlikely to do so.

Multiple Roles of the Private Sector

Civil society plays an important role in health governance as well. Nongovernmental organizations (NGOs) have become an increasingly influential player on the global health scene, and their research and advocacy have had an impact on the formulation of policies and determination of priorities. Medecins Sans Frontieres, for example, a group that raises money primarily on the back of its emergency relief operations, has become a significant advocate for issues ranging from the expansion of treatment services for people affected by AIDS to the development of new drugs for the so-called "neglected diseases." The last are tropical diseases that are not important problems in industrialized countries and for which a profitable commercial market for therapeutic drugs therefore does not exist.

Private foundations also have had an important role in determining the direction of global public health programs, but recent developments have shaken, or at least have demonstrated the potential to shake, the architecture of global health governance to its foundations. The recent gift of more than $30 billion from Warren Buffet to the already enormously endowed Bill and Melinda Gates Foundation means that about $3 billion in grants will eventually be made each year in the global health area, if the foundation remains true to its funding history. Compare that to the WHO budget figures cited above. There is no question that the Gates Foundation, even before its new windfall, had exerted an important, mainly positive, influence on global health priorities by spending large sums on specific areas of research, especially the development of new vaccines, and on innovative public-private sector partnerships such as the Global Fund for AIDS, Tuberculosis, and Malaria (GFATM) and the Global Alliance for Vaccines and Immunization (GAVI). Given the size of its budget, the Gates Foundation will have enormous influence in determining future directions of global health activities. On the other hand, questions already are being raised as to whether the foundation, or any other private entity for that matter, will have the patience for the more plodding, bureaucratic processes of the United Nations agencies and, even more important, of the national governments with which it will have to partner. Developing countries, especially, will require considerable assistance to develop the management and distribution systems that will be needed to deliver the new and existing products, mostly drugs and vaccines, that will be made available to them through the largesse of the Gates Foundation and other recently developed entities.

On the subject of drugs and vaccines, mention needs to be made of the real elephant on the table of global public health—the commercial sector, especially the pharmaceutical companies. If the total WHO budget is on the order of $1 billion a year and that of the Bill and Melinda Gates Foundation is on the order of $3 billion a year, it is certainly worth noting that sales revenues of Pfizer Corporation were about $40 billion in 2003 and that the combined revenues from product sales of the fifty largest pharmaceutical companies total about one-half trillion dollars a year. Yet, probably because of differences in motivation, the public sector and private interests historically have not had a close, collaborative relationship—to the contrary, the relationship frequently has been contentious and adversarial. To some extent, that relationship is changing and changing rapidly, brokered to some degree by the newer actors in the field. Innovative funding mechanisms that serve to lower the risks inherent in new product development are being proposed, and commercial manufacturers seem genuinely more interested in pursuing global public health priorities, as long as they can be assured of a reasonable degree of financial security.

In addition, the commercial sector has some comparative advantages in many areas, including production, marketing, distribution, and, indeed, in governance itself. For the most part, it seems fair to assert that corporate governance is generally more efficient and more effective than what has been seen in the public health sector to date.

The Rise of Partnerships

Those who work in global public health have long insisted that their work is of such fundamental importance that others should pay attention. They have tried to convince others that economic growth depends, at least to a degree, on improved health; that stronger health systems are visible manifestations of increasingly democratic societies; and even that the humanitarian aspects of providing improved health services in a more equitable manner will contribute to national, regional, and global security. They have insisted that global health traditionally has been underfunded and given lower priority than it merits by donor governments and by the private sector. In some ways, they have now won their battle. In no way is global health still the domain of physicians and other traditional "health professionals." Now, politicians, lawyers, economists, sociologists, management experts, and many, many others all participate in the prioritization of public health programs and in their implementation. And with all these new players on the scene, there has been a natural tendency to try to work together—to form partnerships. The number of new public-public and public-private partnerships that have sprung up over the past decade is truly impressive.

The most well known of these partnerships are probably UNAIDS, a new (1995) UN agency in which all of the other UN agencies involved in controlling the HIV/AIDS pandemic participate, and the Global Fund for AIDS, Tuberculosis, and Malaria, a private Swiss foundation with a multibillion dollar endowment. UNAIDS was created, to a certain degree, because of the growing recognition that WHO, as the representative, in fact if not in theory, of the ministries of health of its member states, could not embrace the broad array of disciplines that would be necessary to stem the tide of the epidemic. GFATM was created after a call by the G-8 in 2000 for an innovative, fast-acting financing mechanism to raise and disburse funds for control of its target diseases; existing mechanisms were felt to be excessively bureaucratic and cumbersome. Of course, it was intended to complement, not to duplicate, the efforts of existing agencies. Still, although most other major funders of health programs contributed, sometimes generously, to these new organs, they also developed or maintained their own HIV/AIDS control programs. So the World Bank, subjected to criticism for not taking sufficient action to address the pandemic, developed its Multilateral AIDS Program (MAP), and the U.S. government, for similar reasons, developed the President's Emergency Plan for HIV/AIDS Relief (PEPFAR). Together with the WHO program on HIV/AIDS, these entities try to coordinate their efforts. If they try hard, they may be able, in the end, to develop a satisfactory working relationship and a clear and reasonably respectful understanding of each other's role and so minimize duplication of effort. But the multiplicity of programs, each with its own channels and rules of accountability, make life difficult for recipient countries.

GAVI is another leading example of a public-private sector initiative. Its partners include UNICEF, WHO, the Bill and Melinda Gates Foundation, the World Bank, vaccine manufacturers, NGOs, research institutions, and, of course, developing countries. Its financing arm, the GAVI Fund, provides successful applicants (countries) with the means to raise vaccination coverage to the highest levels, including by providing funds for the purchase of vaccines. GAVI is intended, as are other partnerships, to be complementary rather than duplicative, and it has been at the forefront in developing innovative financing mechanisms that remain, to date, relatively unencumbered by political or procedural entanglements.

As might be inferred from the discussion above, there has been a tendency among donors to form a new organizational entity when a particular agency, such as WHO, has proved to be inadequate, in one or more ways, in discharging its responsibilities in an efficient or effective manner or has taken actions judged to be unsuccessful. Without question, the reexamination of traditional global public health practices has resulted in the development of new, probably better, ways by which health care, both preventive and curative, can be provided. Innovative funding mechanisms, unfettered processes for rapid program implementation, and greater participation by a broader array of parties with a significant interest in program outcomes have been developed, and more should be encouraged.

Toward an Effective System of Global Health Governance

The new global architecture has arisen as a relatively rapid response to deficiencies in the old system; it was not designed from the ground up. It therefore has some of the deficiencies that naturally appear when design efforts are based on a desire to plug existing gaps. As the empty spaces in the global health landscape are progressively filled, attention will have to be paid to many of the cross-cutting functions fundamental to the design of an effective system of governance, including the following:

—*Norm-setting.* WHO traditionally has been recognized as the agency responsible for the establishment of technical guidelines. But new guidelines pertaining to financing, accountability, performance, and participation may be needed.

—*Dispute settlement.* In the new system, it is becoming clear that increased levels of financing and a more "businesslike" relationship between donor agencies and recipients can lead to decisions to interrupt grants or contracts, resulting in a significant negative impact on the health of the target population. A system for resolving disputes that does not result in deterioration of the public health should be developed.

—*Data collection and analysis.* Each of the new agencies and partnerships, as well as the old, has a need for its own data. But data collection requirements run the very real risk of burdening developing countries with redundant and unessential reporting exercises. Coherence in this area would be most welcome. The relatively newly formed Health Metrics Network, intended to strengthen the health information systems in developing countries, may help.

Much has been accomplished, and much more remains to be accomplished. If the global health system is to continue to make progress, some reflection on what might be an ideal system of global health governance is in order. How should priorities be established? How should they be addressed? What agencies or institutions are essential to meeting contemporary and especially future global public health needs? Who should decide these questions, in what forums? Global health has become at least a partial concern of the political establishment, but partial solutions will not help. Strong consideration by global leaders should be given to developing an efficient and just process of global health governance that addresses the needs and desires of all of those who have become involved.

8

Global Environmental Governance

DANIEL C. ESTY

W hile a great deal of attention has been paid to the need for reform of international financial institutions such as the World Bank and the International Monetary Fund, there is an even greater need for reform of global governance in the environmental domain. Trade liberalization, economic integration, and development to support poverty alleviation all require a degree of global governance. Economic interdependence creates a clear logic for structured nation-to-nation cooperation based on the premise of shared gains from enhanced trade as well as the promise of greater peace and stability in a world where economic aspirations are being met.

Investing in governance structures to manage international environmental relations has an equally compelling logic. Pollution does not stop at national borders, and a number of critical natural resources, including the oceans and the atmosphere, are shared by all. The theoretical problem is straightforward. Basic economics teaches that unregulated natural resources are at risk of overexploitation. Fish stocks, for instance, can be run down under "open access" conditions as every fisherman tries to catch as many fish as possible as quickly as possible. Similarly, transboundary spillovers of pollution (such as sulfur dioxide emissions that drift downwind and cause acid rain or contamination of shared rivers like the Danube), if not controlled, become uninternalized externalities—harms for which the polluter does not fully pay. These "market failures" lead to allocative inefficiency, reduced gains from trade, and lost social welfare, not to mention environmental degradation. Providing environmental protection at the supranational scale thus represents one of the most pressing global challenges.[1]

A functioning international environmental regime must address a number of looming threats: climate change, the deterioration of the earth's ozone layer, depletion of fisheries in all of the world's oceans, loss of biodiversity, and the spread of bioaccumulative toxics and heavy metals. Advances in a range of ecological sciences continue to unveil new threats to the "global commons" that deserve attention, including airborne mercury, damaged coral reefs, and disrupted hydrological systems.

In an economically interdependent world, collective action is required to address externalities at the scale on which they arise. Because some environmental problems are transboundary in scale, they cannot be adequately addressed by national governments acting on their own. Stronger national or local environmental laws and programs are useful, but they cannot substitute for sound global governance and international cooperation in response to transboundary spillovers of pollution and the depletion or degradation of the shared resources of the global commons. In the face of a number of inescapably supranational challenges, a governance structure to facilitate international cooperation and confront issues of a global scale becomes essential.[2]

Simply put, ecological interdependence is a fact. What is at issue is whether the world's nations will manage their intertwined fates thoughtfully, explicitly, and effectively—or in an unsystematic and ad hoc manner.

The Existing International Environmental Regime

The existing international environmental regime, anchored by the UN Environment Program (UNEP) in Nairobi, is performing poorly and appears dysfunctional in important respects. Dissatisfaction with the current regime abounds among politicians, business people, environmentalists, and the general public on issues ranging from its halting efforts to understand and confront the prospect of climate change to its inability to respond to questions about food made with genetically modified organisms. Some of its current failings can be attributed to a history of management shortcomings and bureaucratic entanglements, but other aspects of the problem are deeper and more structural.

Fundamentally, the focus and design of the global environmental governance regime predate a full appreciation of the international scope of pollution issues. Hampered by a narrow mandate, a modest budget, and limited political support, UNEP competes with more than a dozen other UN bodies, including the Commission on Sustainable Development (CSD), the UN Development Program (UNDP), the World Meteorological Organization (WMO), and the International Oceanographic Commission (IOC), on the international environmental scene. Adding to the fragmentation are the independent secretariats established under numerous treaties, including the Montreal Protocol (ozone layer protection), the Basel Convention (hazardous waste trade), the Convention on International Trade in Endangered Species (CITES), and the Climate Change Convention, all contending for limited government time, attention, and resources. The lack of a rationalized structure can be seen in many arenas. For example, UNEP, UNDP, the CSD, and the WMO—as well as the Organization for Economic Cooperation and Development (OECD) and the World Bank—all maintain climate change programs, with little coordination and no strategic division of labor. With all of these entities, stretched from Bonn to Montreal and from Nairobi to Geneva, focus is dissipated, efforts splintered, responsibilities scattered, funding squandered, and accountability lost. Priorities are not set in a systematic fashion, nor are budgets coordinated or optimized.

The concerns addressed by these bodies are wide-ranging and diverse. But the response to diversity need not be disorganization. A carefully constructed institutional design with a streamlined, coherent, and comprehensive approach to worldwide environmental challenges has much to offer. Relocation of the core elements of the existing international environmental programs to a single city (one that is near a transportation hub and other UN bodies, that enjoys political stability and minimal corruption, that has modern and cost-effective telecommunications, and that is located in an area that attracts first-rate staff, in a host country that is committed to the success of the enterprise) would greatly enhance efficiency and permit a range of synergies. "One-stop shopping" would be a particular boon to developing countries, many of which are thinly staffed and overstretched as they try to keep up with the vast number of environmental entities, meetings, negotiations, and activities spanning the planet.

Directions for Reform

While the need for institutional reform on the global environmental scene is broadly recognized, there remains considerable disagreement about what direction any restructuring should take. An important group of countries, led by France and Germany, has recently argued for creating a UN Environment Organization (UNEO) by bolstering the current international regime under UNEP. Their proposal calls for upgrading the formal status of UNEP from a UN program to a UN specialized agency (thus putting it on an institutional par with, for example, WHO and UNESCO), reforming UNEP's governing structure, and assessing financial contributions from governments. The Franco-German proposal, however, falls short of the broad-based reform that many observers believe is needed. Constrained in its scope and scale, it builds on the existing weak framework, which has been underperforming for thirty years.

Other observers argue that creating a new global environmental organization (GEO)—or, perhaps more modestly, a global environmental mechanism (GEM)—would provide a better starting point for successful international global environmental governance. An effective GEO need not be a big, new bureaucracy. To the contrary, a streamlined agency that consolidates many of the fragmented environmental activities of the entities identified above, supported by a decentralized network of outside experts (national government officials, academics, business and NGO leaders), would make more sense.

The Commission on Sustainable Development and existing environmental treaty secretariats might all be incorporated into the new structure. With a "global policy network" as its core and a modern organizational design that takes advantage of the technologies of the Information Age, such a GEO could move quickly on breaking issues, bring analytical rigor to hard problems, and take an entrepreneurial approach to developing worldwide response strategies—all with much lower overhead than traditional international organizations.

A functioning GEO would engage not only governments, but also civil society at large, including business and NGO leaders. A vibrant and narrowly focused new organization could provide the information and analytic foundation required for good environmental decisionmaking; the capacity to gauge and compare risks, costs, benefits, and policies; a mechanism for leveraging private sector and government resources deployed at the international level; and a means for improving the results from global-scale environmental spending and programs.[3]

In revitalizing global environmental governance, *focus* must be the watchword. UNEP has gotten bogged down in undertaking projects in dozens of countries. While independently worthy, these local, issue-oriented activities should be undertaken by national governments or local agencies, supported by UNDP or the World Bank. Priority, instead, should be given to two core roles: promoting cooperation in response to inescapably international problems, including management of the oceans, atmosphere, and other resources of the global commons; and providing a convening authority for information sharing in response to common (but not shared) problems, such as water, waste management, and local air pollution, where exchange of data and the identification and dissemination of best practices would pay significant dividends.

The design and architecture of a new global environmental organization should emphasize:

—*Norm creation.* A revised environmental regime would need to offer a forum for the development of international norms, guidelines, and, where necessary, binding rules. In that regard, it might draw on the OECD as a model for norm creation and the WTO as a model for providing a forum for negotiations.

—*Dispute settlement.* The new body should provide a mechanism for settling disputes among countries that relate to shared natural resources or pollution spillover. The dispute settlement mechanisms of the WTO as well as those embodied in a number of other trade agreements provide a useful starting point for institutional design.

—*Data collection and analysis.* Recognizing the enormous opportunities created by the Information Age, the new organization should have a central role in data collection and analysis on a global scale. By helping to spot problems, track trends, and benchmark performance, the organization would be able to provide guidance on how best to address problems at the supranational scale and to support improved practices at the national and local levels.

—*Information exchange.* Building on its data collection role, the new organization would be well positioned to provide analysis of problems and help in evaluating best practices with regard to policy, procedures, and technologies. The work of the OECD as a forum for countries to gather and "compare notes" might serve as a model.

—*Partnerships.* As a forum for international cooperation, a GEO would also be able to support partnerships aimed at developing and disseminating technology as well as at developing cross-border responses to global environmental obligations. The new body might well be able to subsume some of the work of the "clean development mechanism" of the United Nations Framework Convention on Climate Change; ideas that have been developed for further joint implementation of greenhouse gas control strategies; and efforts to develop funding mechanisms to support developing country participation in international environmental agreements.

The effectiveness of any new global environmental organization depends not only on its architecture but also on the processes and procedure adopted. Any new GEO would need to adopt "good governance" principles and practices to ensure that its activities reflect a commitment to both legitimacy and efficacy.[4] Its procedures would need to be transparent, promote public participation, include mechanisms to ensure accountability, provide advance links to expert opinion, and provide mechanisms for structured review and cross-checking of any decisions advanced. It is increasingly clear that public support for international cooperative efforts and global governance more generally depend on careful institutional design and procedural rigor.

Some in the global "South" have held recent attempts to reform global environmental institutions hostage to their demands for a new international economic order. While the underlying question of equity deserves attention, obstructing progress toward better global environmental governance cannot be condoned. More important, good governance principles can help to promote equity through due process, a requirement that minority points of view be heard, increased public participation, and transparency of governing processes. To enable a balance of efficacy, effectiveness, and equity, the new organization must focus its activities with punctilious attention to the dictates of good governance.

Ultimately, the logic of a GEO is quite straightforward. In a globalizing world, finding thoughtful ways to manage international ecological interdependence is imperative. Without a concerted effort to address transboundary pollution spillovers systematically and to use the shared resources of the global commons responsibly, success is impossible. Ensuring an optimal level of international environmental protection, like any other public good, will always be problematic given the challenges of establishing effective collective action.[5] Garnering support for global public goods is even harder because of the international coordination that is required and the ease with which those who wish to "free ride" can escape bearing a share of the burden.

However fraught with difficulty institutional reform may be, the alternative—failure to respond to global-scale pollution challenges and natural resource management issues—is worse. The existing international environmental system can only be described as woefully inadequate. UNEP and the patchwork of other UN bodies, treaty secretariats, and commissions with environmental mandates are buckling under the weight of their current responsibilities while demands for global-scale action are rising. It is time to reengineer the regime, aiming for a new, sleeker, and more efficient design and a rigorous process that will better serve environmental, governmental, public, and business needs.

Notes

1. I use the term *supranational* to encompass both global governance (involving all countries) and international governance (involving two or more nations working together).

2. See Daniel C. Esty, "Good Governance at the Supranational Scale: Globalizing Administrative Law," *Yale Law Journal* 115, no. 7 (2006).

3. See Daniel C. Esty and Maria H. Ivanova, "Revitalizing Global Environmental Governance: A Function-Driven Approach," in *Global Environmental Governance: Options and Opportunities*, edited by Daniel C. Esty and Maria H. Ivanova (Yale University, School of Forestry and Environmental Studies, 2002), pp.181–203.

4. Ibid.

5. See Mansur Olson, *The Logic of Collective Action* (Harvard University Press, 1965).

9

Global Governance Reform: Conclusions and Implications

COLIN I. BRADFORD JR. AND JOHANNES F. LINN

The principal concern of this volume is that the international system comprising both international institutions and global summit-level steering groups is inadequate to meet the challenges of the twenty-first century. Most of today's international institutions were founded in the mid-twentieth century. They were based on the global challenges and power configurations that existed following World War II, when colonialism still reigned, the United States dominated the war-damaged industrial countries, and the cold war began to create divides between East and West. Today, the world is more integrated, and the divisions of colonialism and the cold war are matters of the past. Given their dramatically increased shares of world trade and economic growth, the emerging market economies are rightly claiming a greater voice in decisions made by international institutions. No longer are the challenges facing the globe, unlike those of sixty years ago, the separate domains of specialized disciplines, professions, and institutions. They are interrelated, interactive, and intersectoral, and they demand more integrated and interinstitutional approaches.

But the conditions at the beginning of the twenty-first century do not seem ripe for any major systemic breakthroughs that would replace current structures and create new institutions. The vision and sense of urgency, the innovative spirit, and the leadership that brought the IMF and the World Bank into being at Bretton Woods in 1944 and created the United Nations in San Francisco in 1945 are not present today. Instead, the most feasible path to international reform seems to be to address global governance and substantive policy reforms within individual international institutions while simultaneously reforming global consultative and decisionmaking forums such as summits, in the hope of redirecting and reenergizing the dynamics of the international system through the synergistic and cumulative impact of the reforms undertaken.

The Nexus of Global Reforms

The main conclusion of this book and the discussions on which the chapters are based is precisely that individual institutional reforms in the IMF, the World Bank, and the United Nations—and in global health and environmental governance—are critical, but they are not sufficient to sustain themselves or to achieve the broader goal of increasing the effectiveness of the international system as a whole in dealing with today's challenges. Reform of the overarching global governance groups, especially the G-8 summit but also other regional and sectorial forums, is necessary if change is to be systemic, sufficient, and effective. It is this nexus of global reforms—the interaction and interdependence of individual institutional reforms and broader governance reforms—that defines the global governance reform agenda today.

The story is complicated by conflicting needs and global politics in the international community. On one hand, there is the need to recognize the substantial shifts in the relative economic, demographic, and political weight of nations in the global system—and hence the need to give greater voice and vote to the large emerging market economies in order to increase their influence, participation, and responsibility in managing world affairs. On the other hand, the smaller, poorer nations should not be left out or assigned a minor role in a system that favors the already powerful. Yet increasing the number of seats in the global groups or on the governing boards of institutions creates problems of efficiency and effectiveness. If anything, the global governance system needs to be streamlined to be effective. Legitimacy rests on the capacity to be both representative and effective, simultaneously.

Such conflicting requirements do not make the path to global reform an obvious or an easy one. No uniform solutions have appeared that can be applied throughout the system. Rather, the hope is that the combination of a variety of reforms and their cumulative effects across a broad range of institutions and groups will generate new channels for interests, ideas, and influence that will improve both the capacity of the system and its political governance, increasing in turn both its effectiveness and its representativeness. That is the imperative of the global governance reform agenda today.

The issue of conflicting challenges is well illustrated by reform in the IMF. The reform strategy decided on by the IMF board of governors in Singapore in September 2006 commits the board to reexamining the formula for determining voting power on the IMF executive board in order to give greater weight to selected large emerging market economies. In order to increase the weight of the smaller, poorer countries, IMF members also propose to achieve at least a doubling of the weight of "basic votes" (the equal number of votes given to all countries regardless of their size) in determining voting shares. This two-pronged strategy is not only the kind of expedient political compromise needed to sustain support for the reform effort in the IMF but also the kind of reform necessary to combine efficiency with equity and thereby enhance both the legitimacy and the effectiveness of the institution.

Viewing the network of individual international institutions and global governance groups together as a system should facilitate the reform process by making it possible to exploit synergies and reinforce elements of reform. It also may help further the understanding that not all values and objectives can be fulfilled in each part of the system. In a complex world, the combined effects of reforms throughout the system and the new interactions that they stimulate may provide more complete realization of the goals of reform than isolated intrainstitutional reforms. As Jack Boorman argues in chapter 1, pursuing principles for governance reform across the board—principles such as universality, legitimacy (fairness), subsidiarity, efficiency, and accountability— pushes those values forward in each institution and also helps ensure that the system as a whole maximizes their achievement.

Focusing on the nexus of institutional and global reforms also helps accentuate the potential gains to be had from reinforcing elements. For example, in the Per Jacobsson Lecture of September 2005, Michel Camdessus, former managing director of the IMF, argued that the International Monetary and Financial Committee (IMFC), the interministerial committee guiding the IMF, should be transformed from an advisory body to a decisionmaking group—from a committee to a council—with a membership that is more "congruent" with that of "a global governance group." Camdessus proposes a similar change in the World Bank's interministerial Development Committee. We would add to his proposals the recommendation that the two new councils be combined into one to add still greater "congruence" and efficiency in global financial and development leadership. Camdessus concluded by making an important point—that "far from leading to an undue politicization of the two institutions, this would place responsibilities squarely where they belong, namely, with governments."[1] According to Camdessus, the transformation of the IMFC and the Development Committee, accompanied by broadening of the country composition of the G-8 summits, "could be a good way to address properly the broader issue of world economic governance, far from the illusion of promoting some utopian world government, but with the more limited but necessary, ambition of finding a global response to inescapable global problems."[2] These proposals illustrate the potential of simultaneous reforms in institutions and global groups to reinforce one another, making both more effective. They also illustrate the primacy of top-level national government authorities in giving strategic direction to the international institutions.

Global Governance Reforms and National Leadership

The central locus for democratic legitimacy is the people. The legitimacy to represent the people in an international forum—what we might refer to as representational legitimacy—is most clearly lodged in national political authorities, in particular in the head of state. While there are flaws in that formulation, no other criterion competes successfully with the legitimacy of national leaders based on the support of their people.[3] That is clearly the criterion underlying the Camdessus reforms, which are intended "to make more explicit the real political responsibility" of national leaders in the international system.[4] The secretary-general of the United Nations, the president of the World Bank, the managing director of the IMF, and other appointed leaders do not have the same degree or kind of legitimacy as do leaders of national governments. As a result, global governance reform cannot be based solely on empowering appointed leaders or on getting them to work more closely together.

The fate of the international system depends to a large degree on the vision and statesmanship of prominent national leaders. The Roosevelts and Churchill forged the United Nations; Truman pushed through the formation of the World Bank and the IMF; Valéry Giscard d'Estaing and Helmut Schmidt started the G-7 summits; and a long string of French leaders from Robert Schumann to Jacques Delors took the lead in the gradual formation of the European Union. Today, visionary leadership with respect to the international community is not evident among most of the current leaders of major countries. In any event, in our view it is not clear that making conceptual leaps to a new system with new institutions is the most desirable or necessary, let alone feasible, path to reform. But if the primary site for global reform is indeed the nexus between institutional and global reforms, then what is required now is a group of countries whose leaders are willing and able to push the global reform agenda across both venues. The key question then is this: Is there such a group?

Here are some of our impressions of the political scenario, derived from more than two years of research, consultation, and engagement with officials from major countries.[5] Two industrial countries stand out as the major advocates and practitioners of multilateralism: Canada and Australia. Canada has a long tradition, going back at least to former prime ministers Lester Pearson and Pierre Trudeau, of making multilateralism the centerpiece of Canadian diplomacy and foreign policy. Its most recent manifestations have been the leadership of former prime minister Paul Martin of the G-20 finance ministers in the group's early stages in the late 1990s and his more recent advocacy of broadening the G-8 by creating an L-20 leaders-level summit group modeled on the G-20 group of ten large emerging market economies and ten industrial countries. Canada continues to be vitally engaged in global reform.

Australia in the last two years has played an exemplary role in leading the IMF reform effort, in the G-20 finance ministers meeting in Beijing in 2005, and its own chairing of the G-20 in 2006; in its role in Singapore at the World Bank–IMF annual meetings, where the first steps toward an IMF reform sequence were taken; and in the annual meeting of the G-20 in Australia in November 2006. The troika leadership principle of the G-20 ensures that Australia will continue its efforts into 2007 at the very least. The Australians and Canadians are highly interested in G-8 summit reform, but their official positions currently are less specific than one might expect, given that the G-20/L-20 idea would give them both seats at the table, while other formulations well might not.

The strongest leading governments in the global "South" with respect to global governance reform appear to us to be Brazil and South Africa. Brazil has long conceived of its national identity and development within the framework of its role in the larger world and in the Latin American region. Its difficult experience in the late 1990s, when the repercussions of the Asian and Russian financial crises threatened its stability, strengthens the assertiveness and visibility of Brazil's finance ministry in discussions of the current pattern of global imbalances and the role of international financial institutions in the global economy. Brazil is also a major player in international trade negotiations and aspires to a seat on the UN Security Council. The October 2006 reelection of President Lula da Silva ensures continuity in Brazil's global leadership. South Africa takes its role as a leading African country extremely seriously; it is careful to present itself in international affairs as a country that attempts to articulate views on behalf of and with the agreement of its African neighbors. The success of the transition from apartheid under Mandela and the visibility of Trevor Manuel in global finance during his long tenure as chair of the Development Committee have strengthened South Africa's role as a leader in the international community. Its role as chair of the G-20 in 2007 will keep it in a visible leadership position for the foreseeable future.

Two Asian countries, Japan and China, have shown some interest in the international reform agenda. The future of Japan's role in world affairs depends on its new political leadership, but its professionalism and experience in international affairs and global finance give it continuing prominence. Japan aspires to a seat on the UN Security Council, and its positions on global financial institutions and summit reforms tend to favor the status quo, which already gives Japan substantial weight. China also exhibits significant interest and presence in global reform discussions, but it is more inclined to wait for an emerging consensus than to put forward concrete proposals or assert leadership. It is more active on security and UN affairs than on the international financial institutions (IFIs) and summits. China is reluctant to be brought into the G-8 by itself, which would put it in a minority position as the only non-industrial country and could possibly jeopardize its relations with the rest of the developing world. In sum, the two largest Asian economies are internationally engaged but not currently playing strong leadership roles. If anything, they have tended to look more toward the strengthening of Asian regional summits and organizations, including the possible creation of an Asian monetary fund.

Two other economic heavyweights, India and Germany, seem to have comparable positions on global reform. Both are significant players on most global issues, and their presence and political weight seem commensurate with their status. But both are more preoccupied with internal issues and governance than with global governance reform. They tend to be quiet and cautious rather than forthcoming and innovative in global discussions, despite the stake each has in its place in the international system. Both aspire to seats on the UN Security Council, but they are not trying to get there by taking a strong role on global issues and institutions in the way that, for example, Brazil and South Africa have. On the other hand, Germany and India seem more seriously attentive and engaged than Korea and Turkey, two countries that hold back even more in the international reform conversation. How Chancellor Angela Merkel manages Germany's leadership of the G-8 summit in 2007 will reveal her hand as a player in the global reform effort.

Weakened political leadership—whether because of expected leadership changes, impending elections, or other reasons—plays a significant role in a number of countries. In the United Kingdom, the transition from Tony Blair to Gordon Brown is under way. Both are prominent international reformers, but the tensions between them seem to have made even quite senior officials under each of them reluctant to engage fully in the global debate on reform, leaving it to their principals to articulate their own views and visions when and where they see fit. The dramatic decline in public support for Jacques Chirac in France has left his government distracted on the international front and reluctant to be fully forthcoming in pushing for reform, preferring instead to protect the position of France in the G-8 and in the IFIs. The election of former EC commissioner Romano Prodi as head of government in Italy is a hopeful sign in terms of global reform, but the delicate balance in his coalition government may weaken his potential on the international front. Indeed, the uncertainty regarding the fate of the constitution of the European Union following its defeat in referendums in France and the Netherlands in the spring of 2005 is a substantial obstacle in the formation of a strong European position and role in global reform.

Finally, there is the United States, undoubtedly the key player in international reform, especially as a gatekeeper in determining which options and issues have any chance of moving forward. Under the George W. Bush administration, the Treasury Department has been a strong and positive player in the IMF reform effort, assuming a noteworthy, important, and commendable role. However, the U.S. position and policy toward reform in the World Bank and the United Nations have been complicated by the difficult presidency so far of Paul Wolfowitz at the bank and the controversial role of John Bolton as U.S. ambassador at the UN. The Bush administration seems to be a reluctant reformer, at best, regarding summits, with the president not appearing to be an enthusiastic summiteer and seeming to prefer smaller, more manageable "coalitions of the willing" to discussions and negotiations in larger arenas involving partners with differing views. A full turn of U.S. foreign policy away from a more unilateralist approach to a fully engaged multilateral presence would seem to have to wait at least until the U.S. elections in November 2008. One of the factors that may be driving the

United States to a more open acknowledgment of the need for governance reform is the fear that the Asian powers may begin to create their own strong regional institutions and forums as a reaction to their underrepresentation in global institutions, especially the IFIs. Such a trend could weaken the existing global governance structure even further and most likely would not be in the U.S. national interest, a fact that appears to be well understood in the current administration.

Other G-20 countries seem to be neutral observers, including Russia, which during the run-up to the St. Petersburg G-8 summit in July 2006 was unwilling or unable to focus on the longer-term institutional reform issues. Mexico has had a trying presidential election and aftermath, which have siphoned off its attention from the global arena. In our experience, Argentina, Indonesia, and Saudi Arabia have been relatively passive players.

Thus we see a mixed picture, with some significant countries showing leadership in pushing for reform while others evidently face constraints on the priority, innovative effort, and leadership that they can give to the reform agenda. However, the global challenges are urgent, and the international institutions need support from member countries to move forward. The key to success seems to be to apply persistent pressure on multiple institutional fronts and on a variety of issues over time in order to exploit every opportunity for action and to leverage every opportunity for change. Given the fact that great leaps forward or breakthroughs are highly unlikely, the most feasible path to reform seems to call for steady effort by a variety of actors—current and former leaders, governments, think tanks, NGOs—on a variety of fronts to upgrade the international system to meet the challenges of the twenty-first century. As with many other areas of political and institutional reform, it may take a serious global crisis to shake the key players out of their current inertia. Certainly, the historic global governance initiatives that followed World War II were an example of crisis providing the impetus for reform. But we would hope that in the absence of visionary leadership, common sense will prevent crises and promote global governance reform at the same time.

National Politics and International Behavior

If the nexus of global reform is the link between institutional reform and global governance, the nexus of power in the new global age now seems to be between domestic politics and international engagement.[6] If national officials are the most legitimate source of political authority, the links of internal politics to foreign policy and international engagement are the nexus of power in international affairs. The different degrees to which individual countries exercise leadership in global reforms, just outlined above, clearly illustrates this nexus. The point we want to emphasize here is that if the essence of globalization is the interpenetration of societies rather than international relations between autonomous nations, then the grounds for domestic political discourse and decisionmaking shift and the links between internal and external issues and policies begin to fuse.

The proposal by IMF managing director Rodrigo de Rato to put financial surveillance of economic policies on a multilateral footing is an excellent example of these shifts in the terrain of international negotiations and their implications for national policymaking in the global context. De Rato's idea of multilateral surveillance envisions a group of countries sitting down with the IMF to review the national economic policies of individual countries from a global perspective instead of continuing the current practice of surveillance, in which senior IMF officials and senior country economic policy officials engage in bilateral discussions.

The first trial run of this proposal is de Rato's initiative to bring five countries together to discuss the current pattern of global imbalances. At the moment, the United States (with its large fiscal and trade deficits) and China (with its large trade and capital account surpluses) are the major players. De Rato has invited the Eurozone, Japan, and Saudi Arabia to join the United States and China (and the IMF) to discuss the nature of global imbalances, different perspectives on their causes, alternative views of their consequences, and ideas for their resolution. This is an important new idea that, if taken seriously by all participants, could become an important mechanism for adjusting national economic policies to meet global requirements and could strengthen the role of the IMF in the global economy as a consequence. It deserves support from the key players, especially the United States and China. The idea might be improved by adding to the group a country, such as Brazil, that experienced the dramatic impact of global imbalances on its domestic economy and international position. Brazil could in effect represent the interests of the rest of the world, which could be significantly affected by how the imbalances between the United States and China are resolved.

The changing nature of the nexus of power between domestic and international policies fuses external and internal interests in a new way. The experiment in multilateral surveillance would be facilitated if countries, especially China and the United States in this case, were to incorporate into their policymaking process consideration of how the global impact of their economic policies affects their own national interests. That is far from standard practice today. Moreover, today debates typically are couched in terms of one country putting blame and pressure on the other—for example, the United States pushing China to move away from its fixed exchange rate and China pushing the United States to correct its fiscal and trade deficits. Instead, each country needs to articulate and execute policy adjustments in relation to its own domestic and international interests. That means that each country needs to base its policy adjustments on the argument that reducing global imbalances are in the domestic interest, enabling it to reap the benefits of sustainable monetary, fiscal, and structural policies and of integration into the global economy. Ultimately, that approach is more politically sustainable and analytically accurate than playing on national public perceptions by blaming or pressuring others.

A good example of unnecessary tensions leading to confrontation rather than coordination arose in the 1980s when, rather than trying to find domestic reasons for making internal adjustments, the United States and Japan blamed each other for the global imbalances prevailing at that time. In fact, in the 1990s, the United States eventually did reduce its fiscal deficit, not to satisfy Japan's interest in U.S. fiscal correction but to lessen pressure on capital markets, thereby lowering interest rates and fueling domestic growth through lower borrowing costs. At times, bashing and blaming others makes for good domestic politics in the short term, but it rarely generates the best policy mix in an interdependent global economy over the long term.

. Another example of the need to maintain a delicate balance between domestic politics and international policies is the movement of European countries toward an increasingly integrated European Union. The defeat of the proposed European Constitution in referendums in the United Kingdom and the Netherlands in the spring of 2005 made it clear that reaching too far toward global integration could lead in a strong and decisive way to the reassertion of domestic political primacy over internationalization. The backlash that occurred reveals the critical need to conceptualize and articulate international policies in terms of domestic priorities and politics rather than purely as desiderata in their own right.

Two further specific examples of the interplay between domestic politics and international policies addressed in earlier chapters of this volume are the reforms needed in IFI governance and in the G-8 summit—by rebalancing shares and chairs in the former and by expanding the range of countries represented in the latter. In both cases, the main challenge is to overcome the resistance to reform of traditional domestic interests, which hope to maintain individual countries' or even individual ministries' influence in the IFIs and the G-8. They must be convinced that reform will improve the legitimacy—that is, the effectiveness and representativeness—of these institutions in a way that is in the long-term national interest even of the traditionally dominant countries, the United States and the European nations. In the remainder of this chapter we will briefly summarize our views on how reform of the IFIs and of the G-8 summit could be propelled forward in a substantive yet pragmatic manner.

Rebalancing the Shares and Chairs in the International Financial Institutions

A core reform issue is the rebalancing of the weight of members in international institutions in light of members' changing economic and demographic weights since World War II and of changes forecast for the coming decades. Prime examples are the World Bank and the IMF, which traditionally are dominated by Europe and the United States. The main problem is twofold. On one hand, by any relevant measure the Europeans clearly are overrepresented in the IFIs, both in shares and chairs, relative to their share in the global economy (let alone population). But they are reluctant to give up any of their rights and privileges, especially since doing so would reduce the role in these institutions of individual countries and specific ministries and could make their continuing financial support of the IFIs more difficult to justify to domestic taxpayers. On the other hand, the United States, which frequently is seen as "the elephant in the room" because it is the largest single shareholder, wields an exceptional right to veto key decisions; moreover, the institutions' headquarters are located in the United States.[7] The United States also has been reluctant to reduce its dominant role in these institutions for fear of reducing its scope for using them as instruments of U.S. foreign policy and for fear of losing support for them in Congress. This preponderance of influence by the traditional powers is now being challenged by the newly emerging economic powers, especially in Asia, where initiatives to set up or strengthen regional financial institutions as alternatives to the traditional global financial institutions have been gaining momentum, partly as a reaction to the lack of progress until very recently in rebalancing shares and chairs within the IFIs.

Despite the extreme difficulty of getting ministries in individual European countries to give up their visibility and direct engagement on the executive boards, a good case actually can be made that the Europeans as a group would strengthen their position in the executive boards of the Bank and the IMF if they were to consolidate the eight chairs currently held by individual European countries and constituencies into a single chair with a combined voting share of more than 25 percent. That would give Europe the largest voting share and veto power, along with the United States. Such a move would also mark a major improvement in governance by reducing the number of seats at the table from twenty-four to as few as seventeen, thereby making the board a more effective decisionmaking body while enhancing European influence at the same time.[8]

To provide incentives for the Europeans to reduce their shares and consolidate their chairs into a single seat, we propose—in the spirit of striking a "grand bargain"—that the United States voluntarily give up its veto in both the IMF and the World Bank. If the United States voluntarily withdrew its right to veto major decisions in exchange for the Europeans consolidating their chairs into one and withdrawing the veto power that would then accrue to Europe, both sides would gain in terms of their key shared objective—making the IFIs more effective instruments of global financial and development policy. Doing so would also give the emerging market economies, especially those from Asia, a stronger voice and vote in the IFIs, thus reducing the pressure for fragmentation of the multilateral financial institutional system into regional blocs.

For the United States the key question is whether it wants to break the momentum of regionalization and support a move toward more effective, legitimate, and truly multilateral financial institutions. The fact is that the U.S. veto, which unilateralizes the U.S. role in the IFIs and creates resistance on the part of other countries, is inconsistent with the essential idea of a multilateral international institution. As IMF historian James Boughton writes in chapter 2 of this volume: "to borrow Thomas Friedman's phrase, the world economy has become a lot flatter since 1944, but to many people the IMF still looks like a steep mountain with the United States sitting at the summit." Worse still, as John Ikenberry recently pointed out, "the critical question for the future is: how will the United States respond to its lost legitimacy as a hegemonic leader?"[9] The unfortunate truth is that increasingly the United States itself is becoming a contentious issue in global affairs rather than the leader of the international community as a whole. For the United States to reduce its role as global lightening rod, it will need to take dramatic steps to modify its foreign policies and its role in international affairs. To regain its role as a leader of nations in a restructured international system, the United States will need to become a leader on behalf of the world. It must lead by virtue of its ability to reflect in its own behavior the values, interests, and views of others rather than to reinstall itself as hegemonic ruler by virtue of its power alone. Renouncing the U.S. veto in the IMF and the World Bank would be a small but significant step in the right direction. It would be an example of reconceptualizing American interests by redefining the U.S. presence in the world in a new way that incorporates the interests of others rather than seeks to prevail over them in both form and substance.

Such a grand bargain between the United States and Europe on chairs and vetoes would give real content and meaning to IFI governance reform. Along with other reforms under consideration, it could transform the spirit of IFI governance from one of resentment of the dominance of the two major powers into one of the multilateral bargaining, coalition building, and more democratic global governance needed for the twenty-first century.

Reforming the G-8 as the Global Apex Institution

The compelling logic for international institutional reform is that the legitimacy and effectiveness of these institutions are undermined by their twentieth-century governance structure, which does not recognize the economic transformations of the last fifty years or the increasing need for representational legitimacy to ensure their effectiveness in the twenty-first century. Extending that rationale to the G-8 summits, it is clear that the constellation of countries in the group are predominantly rich, industrial, Western countries in a world that is predominantly poor, non-industrial, and non-Western. The G-8 embodies parochialism rather than universality as a principle of governance, to pick up on Jack Boorman's set of principles in chapter 1. It has no claim to represent the world or to be a steering committee for meeting global challenges—not in today's world of more than 6 billion people and much less in the world of 9 billion people anticipated for 2050, in which the additional 3 billion people will come from non-Western, nonindustrial, poorer countries. Therefore, the absence of a truly representative, globally inclusive steering group means that there is a void at the apex of the international system.

The international community is composed of a set of international institutions that have their own sectorial governance mechanisms, but there is no global governance group at the apex of the international system that has an overview of the system as a whole and of the interrelationships among the institutions. That may have been appropriate for the twentieth century, when problem solving and professions were based on specialization and expertise alone. The twenty-first century, in which globalization has become the dominant modality and motif of international relationships, is characterized by an interpenetration of domains in which the interconnections among challenges, sectors, and institutions are central rather than peripheral to the management of issues. As a consequence, the void at the apex is now critical. The effectiveness of the international system depends on the relationships among the institutions that constitute it, which are crucial to addressing contemporary challenges.

These relationships present strategic guidance issues, not simple questions of interagency coordination or internal management. Therefore the annual meeting of the heads of international agencies and institutions at the Chief Executives Board (CEB), while welcome as a much-needed operational coordination mechanism, is an inadequate solution to the problem. The interrelationships among institutions are ultimately political problems because they entail determining relative priorities among the areas of health, education, gender equality, the environment, poverty, finance, trade, growth, and security—which in the end are determined by societal values, requiring societal input. Since national officials are the most legitimate source of political authority, heads of state and government are the most optimal representatives for public input and adjudication of cross-sector values, conflicts, and jurisdictions.

In addition, heads of state also are uniquely endowed among national authorities with intersectorial, interministerial, integrated responsibilities for public policy. They alone among political authorities can transcend the boundaries of sectors and bureaucracies to forge integrated strategies for dealing with problems whose essential character is increasingly multidimensional. Health governance issues cannot be resolved by health ministers alone, nor environmental problems by environment ministers alone, nor financial challenges by finance ministers alone. Today the global challenges in each domain are more fundamentally defined by their interaction with factors and forces outside each domain—so that overall strategic guidance is required to address their intersectorial and interinstitutional nature.

There is no better example for illustrating the integrated nature of global challenges than the Millennium Declaration and the Millennium Development Goals. The Millennium Declaration, promulgated by 183 heads of state at the Millennium Summit in September 2000, set out five major baskets of objectives in the areas of security, governance, human rights, poverty, and the environment, making clear their interconnectedness. At the Financing for Development (FFD) summit in Monterrey in March 2002, heads of state endorsed the eight Millennium Development Goals (MDGs) and quantitative indicators for tracking them. The MDGs are now the primary framework for multilateral and bilateral cooperation on development around the world. The MDGs consist of global goals to be achieved by 2015 in the areas of poverty, gender equality, universal education, mortality, infectious diseases, the environment, and international cooperation.

In addition to being specific goals to guide development efforts, the MDGs redefined the development paradigm as an interdependent, multidimensional set of actions, replacing the traditional focus of the development community, which was principally economic and financial in its orientation. The MDGs make clear that poverty reduction will not occur without action on gender, education, health, and environmental issues and that no action in those areas will be sustained unless direct actions are taken to reduce poverty, stimulate economic growth, and improve institutions and governance. The MDGs are one example of why the World Bank, the IMF, the World Trade Organization, the World Health Organization, and other specialized UN agencies need the strategic guidance that only heads of state can provide on how to relate to each other on behalf of a larger, multifaceted, and multi-institutional human agenda.

The void at the apex means that the MDGs and the Millennium Declaration have no steering group, no strategic guidance, and no focal point for implementation that can integrate individual institutional efforts into system-wide mobilization of resources and policy actions. That illustrates but does not exhaust the reasons why the G-8 summit needs to be reconstituted, in terms of both membership and stewardship, to fit the twenty-first century. Of course, one might wish to focus instead on reforming the economic, social, and environmental steering capacity of the UN and in particular aim for a fundamental redirection of the Economic and Social Council (ECOSOC) into an Economic Security Council of the UN. However, the painful experience with UN reform in recent decades, culminating most recently in the failure of the Millennium+5 UN summit in September 2005 to make any headway in UN governance reform (see also chapter 4), leads us to look to a revamped G-8 as the group to provide the necessary political forum for the major powers of the twenty-first century to discuss and, where possible, reach agreement on how to address some of the world's key challenges.

If it is to serve as a legitimate global apex institution, the G-8 needs to be enlarged to include the major emerging market economies in deliberations and decisions on issues that are global in scale and scope. We argue in chapter

5 that taking the ten industrial economies (including the EU) and the ten emerging market economies that are in the G-20 finance ministers group and creating an L-20 leaders-level group to replace the G-8 is one strong, pragmatic option that has salience and relevance. But it is not the only option. Many are convinced that the group should consist of a core consisting of the G-8 plus China, India, Brazil, and South Africa (and some say Mexico), thereby creating an L-12 or L-13. Others consider an L-12 or L-13 plus another half-dozen seats to be filled by different countries, depending on the issues being discussed ("variable geometry"), a better option because it is more inclusive and creates opportunities to bring countries that are neither large nor powerful to the table. Some find regional representation to be an attractive vehicle for inclusion. For us, the bottom line is that the current G-8 is condemned to irrelevance if its membership is not expanded. Some step forward on summit reform needs to be made, and made soon, and any of the alternatives mentioned above look to us substantially better than the status quo. The key requirement is that the new forum be substantially more inclusive, broader in its focus, and based on a new commitment to asserting stewardship of the international system by tackling a few major global challenges and pushing reform of the international institutions as a major priority.

The Way Forward for Global Governance Reform

The main point emerging from this volume is twofold. First, significant structural change in the country composition, mandates, and functions of international institutions and summits is vital to reflect the changing balance among the world's major economies and to address effectively the growing challenges facing our increasingly integrated and rapidly transforming globe. Second, each international institution is no longer able to deal effectively with its primary mandate without strategic guidance and well-defined relationships with other institutions that address related issues outside its primary mandate, mission, and capacity.

The central message of this book is therefore that there is a tight nexus between reform of individual international institutions and reform of the global governance system and its apex institution. Without progress on both fronts the international system will not have the capacity to provide the world's population with adequate responses to the issues of health, education, gender equality, environmental sustainability, poverty reduction, financial stability, economic growth, human rights, good governance, and personal security. If the international system does not develop the capacity to meet the challenges of the global age, it will fail to have "practical meaning," and it will falter and slip behind in meeting humanity's hopes and expectations.

Notes

1. Michel Camdessus, "International Financial Institutions: Dealing with New Global Challenges," Per Jacobsson Lecture, Washington, September 25, 2005 (www.perjacobsson.org/lectures.htm), p. 10.

2. Ibid., p. 12.

3. One obvious flaw is that it fails to deal with the problem of autocratic regimes, whose democratic legitimacy is at best weak. That also weakens the representational legitimacy of their heads of state in international forums.

4. Camdessus, "International Financial Institutions," p. 5.

5. We consulted principally, but not exclusively, with officials and think tank representatives in the G-20 countries.

6. For a definition of the "global age" as an era distinct from the modern age, see Martin Albrow, *The Global Age* (Stanford University Press, 1997).

7. The U.S. veto right derives from the fact that the threshold for passage of major decisions—such as quota increases, changes in the Articles of Agreement, and so forth—is a supermajority of 85 percent and the United States has more than 17 percent of the voting power.

8. An interim step would be to unify only the Eurozone chairs, which would be justified especially in view of their common currency and common monetary and exchange rate policy.

9. G. John Ikenberry, "America and the Reform of Global Institutions," CIGI '06, Centre for International Governance Innovation, Waterloo, Ontario, Canada, July 29, 2006, p. 18.

Contributors

COLIN I. BRADFORD JR. is a nonresident senior fellow in the Brookings Institution's Global Economy and Development program and at the Centre for International Governance Innovation (CIGI) in Waterloo, Canada. Previously he was chief economist and head of donor relations at the U.S. Agency for International Development, and he has held senior policy and economic positions in the Organization for Economic Cooperation and Development in Paris, the World Bank, the U.S. Treasury Department, and the U.S. Senate. He has taught at Yale for ten years and at American University for six years as well as at Georgetown University and at the Johns Hopkins School for Advanced International Studies; he also has published widely on international issues. Over the last ten years, he has played significant roles in the development of the Millennium Development Goals.

JOHANNES F. LINN is the executive director of the Wolfensohn Center for Development and a senior fellow in the Brookings Institution's Global Economy and Development program. He entered the World Bank in the 1970s as a young professional and subsequently worked as a research and operational economist and manager on urban development, on East Asia, and on international economics and country policy assignments. He was staff director of the *World Development Report 1988* on public finance. During 1991–95 he served as a vice president of the World Bank, first for Financial Policy and Resource Mobilization and subsequently for Europe and Central Asia. He has recently been the director of the *UNDP Human Development Report* on regional cooperation in Central Asia.

JACK BOORMAN was for more than eleven years the director of the Policy Development and Review Department of the International Monetary Fund. In the latter years of his career with the fund, he was counselor and special adviser to the managing director. In those capacities he was a frequent participant in IMF International Monetary and Financial Committee (IMFC) meetings. He held several other positions in the fund, including positions in the European and Asian Departments and as resident representative in Indonesia. Before beginning his career in the IMF, he taught at the University of Southern California, from which he received his Ph.D. in economics, and at the University of Maryland. He also served as a financial economist in the Research Department of the Federal Deposit Insurance Corporation. He is the author of a number of books and many papers on diverse topics, including development, structural adjustment, and developing country debt; emerging market country issues; international insolvency; governance; and IMF policies and country operations. He currently serves as adviser to the director of the IMF Independent Evaluation Office and as the chairman of the investment committee of the board of trustees of LeMoyne College, and he continues to write on global governance, emerging markets, and other topics.

JAMES BOUGHTON is historian of the International Monetary Fund, and he has been assistant director in the IMF's Policy Development and Review Department since 2001. From 1981 until he was named historian in 1992, he held various positions in the Research Department. Before joining the IMF staff, he was a professor of economics at Indiana University, and he served as an economist at the Organization for Economic Cooperation and Development in Paris. His publications include five books and numerous articles in professional journals. His latest book, *Silent Revolution*, on the history of the IMF from 1979 to 1989, was published in October 2001. He is currently working on a sequel.

NANCY BIRDSALL is the founding president of the Center for Global Development. Before launching the center, she served for three years as senior associate and director of the Economic Reform Project at the Carnegie Endowment for International Peace. From 1993 to 1998 she was executive vice president of the Inter-American Development Bank. Before that, she spent fourteen years in research, policy, and management positions at the World Bank. She is the author, coauthor, or editor of more than a dozen books and monographs on international development issues.

ANN FLORINI is visiting professor and director of the Centre on Asia and Globalization at the Lee Kuan Yew School of Public Policy at the National University of Singapore. She is also a senior fellow in the Brookings Institution's Foreign Policy Studies program. Her research focuses on new approaches to global governance, including the roles of civil society and the private sector in addressing global issues. Currently she is examining governance in the energy sector. She is author or editor of three books on governance, civil society, and globalization and has published numerous journal articles, monographs, book chapters, and other publications.

CARLOS PASCUAL is vice president of Foreign Policy Studies at the Brookings Institution. He joined Brookings after a twenty-three year career in the U.S. State Department, National Security Council, and the U.S. Agency for International Development. Most recently he was the Department of State coordinator for reconstruction and stabilization, focusing on societies in transition from conflict or civil strife, and coordinator for U.S. assistance to Europe and Eurasia. From 2000 to 2003, he served as U.S. ambassador to Ukraine. In the 1990s he held a variety of positions in the NSC and USAID dealing with Russia, eastern Europe, and Eurasia, including two years as special assistant to the president of the United States for Russia, Ukraine, and Eurasia.

ALEXANDER SHAKOW joined the World Bank in 1981 after a nineteen-year career in senior U.S. government positions, including Peace Corps director for Indonesia and assistant administrator for policy and program at USAID. In twenty-one years with the World Bank, he held a number of key policy positions, including director of external affairs and, from 1995 until his retirement in 2002, executive secretary of the World Bank–IMF Development Committee. Since that time he has carried out a number of consulting assignments for the World Bank; the Global Fund to Fight AIDS, TB and Malaria; and the Food and Agriculture Organization.

DR. RONALD WALDMAN is a physician with substantial experience and expertise in public health in complex emergencies, child health in developing countries, medical epidemiology, and infectious and communicable diseases, including malaria and cholera. Most recently he has been professor of clinical population and family health and the director of the Program on Forced Migration and Health at the Mailman School of Public Health at Columbia University. He is on the board of directors of Physicians for Human Rights, and he is a member of the board of overseers of the International Rescue Committee.

DANIEL C. ESTY is the Hillhouse Professor at Yale University, with faculty appointments in both the School of Forestry and Environmental Studies and the Law School. He is also director of the Yale Center for Environmental Law and Policy and the Yale World Fellows Program. From 1989–93, he served in a variety of positions at the U.S. Environmental Protection Agency, including special assistant to the EPA administrator, deputy chief of staff of the agency, and deputy assistant administrator for policy. He is author or editor of nine books and numerous articles on environmental policy issues.

Index